TEACHER'S PET PUBLICATIONS

PUZZLE PACK
for
The Old Man and the Sea

based on the book by
Ernest Hemingway

Written by
William T. Collins

© 2005 Teacher's Pet Publications
All Rights Reserved

The materials in this packet are copyrighted
by Teacher's Pet Publications, Inc.

These pages may be duplicated by the purchaser
for use in the purchaser's own classroom.

Copying any of these materials and distributing them
for any other purpose is a violation of the copyright laws.

© 2005 Teacher's Pet Publications, Inc.
www.tpet.com

INTRODUCTION
If you already own the LitPlan for this title, this Puzzle Pack will refresh your Unit Resource Materials and Vocabulary Resource Materials sections plus give you additional materials you can substitute into the tests. If you do not already have a complete LitPlan, these pages will give you some supplemental materials to use with your own plan. There are two main groups of materials: one set for unit words (such as characters' names, symbols, places, etc.) and one set for vocabulary words associated with the book.

WORD LIST
There is a word list for both the unit words and the vocabulary words. These lists show you which words are being used in the materials and the clues or definitions being used for those words. You may want to give students a word list with clues/definitions to help them, or you may want students to only have a word list (without clues/definitions) if you want them to work a little harder. Both are available for duplication. The word lists can also be your "calling key" for the bingo games.

FILL IN THE BLANK AND MATCHING
There are 4 each of the fill in the blank and matching worksheets for both the unit and vocabulary words. These pages can be used either as extra worksheets for students or as objective parts of a unit test. They can be done individually if students need extra help or as a whole class activity to review the material covered.

MAGIC SQUARES
The magic squares not only reinforce the material covered but also work on reasoning and math skills. Many teachers have told us that their students really enjoy doing these!

WORD SEARCH PUZZLES
The word search words go in all directions, as indicated on your answer keys. Two of the word search puzzles have the clues listed rather than the words. This makes the puzzle a little more difficult, but it reinforces the material better. Two word search puzzles have words only for students who find the clue puzzles too difficult.

CROSSWORD PUZZLES
Both unit and vocabulary word sections have 4 crossword puzzles.

BINGO CARDS
There are 32 individual bingo cards for the unit words and 32 individual bingo cards for the vocabulary words. You can use your word list as a "call list," calling the words at random and marking them off of your list as you go, or you could use the flash cards by cutting them apart and drawing the words at random from a hat (or box or whatever). To make a better review, you might ask for the definition and spelling of each word as you call it out–or you could call out the definitions and have students tell you the words they need to look for on the puzzle.

JUGGLE LETTERS
The vocabulary juggle letter game is intended to help students learn the spellings of the words. One sheet has the definitions listed on it as an extra help for students who need it or to reinforce the definitions if you choose to do so.

FLASH CARDS
We've included a set of vocabulary flash cards you can duplicate, cut, and fold for your students. Some teachers make a few sets for general use by the class; others make a set for each student. Some teachers duplicate them for each student and have the students cut & fold their own. You can cut out just the words and put them in a hat, have each student pick out one word and write the definition and a sentence for that word. Students then swap words and papers, with the next student adding a sentence of his own under the last one. You can have students swap as many times as you like. Each time the student will read the sentences written prior to his own and then add a sentence. You can cut out the words and definitions separately and play "I Have; Who Has?" Each student in the room draws a word and definition. The first student says, "I have (the name of the word). Who has the definition?" The student with the definition reads it then says, "I have (the name of the vocabulary word she has). Who has the definition?" The round continues until all words and definitions have been given.

The Old Man and The Sea Word List

No.	Word	Clue/Definition
1.	BAIT	Fish lure
2.	BAT	Baseball club
3.	BONITO	Kind of tuna
4.	BROTHERS	The fish are our ____.
5.	CAMPEON	The old man: El ___
6.	CARCASS	Leftover bones
7.	CLUB	Santiago hit the sharks with one.
8.	CRAMPS	Santiago's muscular problem with his hands
9.	CUBA	Santiago's home country
10.	DEFEAT	Loss
11.	DIMAGGIO	Baseball great
12.	DOLPHIN	Second kind of fish Santiago ate
13.	EXACT	It is better to be lucky. But I would rather be ____
14.	EYE	Santiago got a cut below his ____ when the fish pulled him over.
15.	FLYING	Santiago ate ____ fish from the bigger fish's stomach.
16.	GAFF	Large hook with which one pulls in a lined fish
17.	HARPOON	Sharp instrument that finally killed the big fish
18.	LIONS	Subject of the old man's dreams
19.	LUCK	Santiago had a streak of bad ____
20.	MANOLIN	The boy
21.	MARLIN	Kind of fish the old man caught
22.	MARTIN	Pub/restaurant owner
23.	MAST	It holds a sail.
24.	NETS	Tied rope-like things that catch fish
25.	NEWSPAPER	Daily news publication
26.	OAR	Santiago tied his knife to one to make a weapon.
27.	PEDRICO	He received the head of the fish from Santiago
28.	RICE	Yellow ____; a friendly, wishful joke
29.	SALAO	The worst kind of bad luck
30.	SANTIAGO	El Campeon; the old man
31.	SEA	Ocean
32.	SHACK	Small house, usually run-down
33.	SHARKS	They attacked and ate the big fish.
34.	SKIFF	Santiago's kind of boat
35.	TOWED	What the big fish did to Santiago's boat
36.	TRICKS	I know many ____ and I have resolution.
37.	WET	The fish's splash got Santiago all ____.
38.	WRESTLING	Santiago got his nickname from arm ____ in his youth.

The Old Man and The Sea Fill In The Blanks 1

1. I know many ____ and I have resolution.
2. Second kind of fish Santiago ate
3. Large hook with which one pulls in a lined fish
4. Pub/restaurant owner
5. Leftover bones
6. Baseball club
7. It holds a sail.
8. Santiago had a streak of bad ____
9. Santiago ate ____ fish from the bigger fish's stomach.
10. The worst kind of bad luck
11. Daily news publication
12. Sharp instrument that finally killed the big fish
13. Santiago tied his knife to one to make a weapon.
14. They attacked and ate the big fish.
15. Santiago got his nickname from arm ____ in his youth.
16. The fish's splash got Santiago all ____.
17. El Campeon; the old man
18. Santiago's home country
19. The old man: El ___
20. Baseball great

The Old Man and The Sea Fill In The Blanks 1 Answer Key

TRICKS	1. I know many ____ and I have resolution.
DOLPHIN	2. Second kind of fish Santiago ate
GAFF	3. Large hook with which one pulls in a lined fish
MARTIN	4. Pub/restaurant owner
CARCASS	5. Leftover bones
BAT	6. Baseball club
MAST	7. It holds a sail.
LUCK	8. Santiago had a streak of bad ____
FLYING	9. Santiago ate ____ fish from the bigger fish's stomach.
SALAO	10. The worst kind of bad luck
NEWSPAPER	11. Daily news publication
HARPOON	12. Sharp instrument that finally killed the big fish
OAR	13. Santiago tied his knife to one to make a weapon.
SHARKS	14. They attacked and ate the big fish.
WRESTLING	15. Santiago got his nickname from arm ____ in his youth.
WET	16. The fish's splash got Santiago all ____.
SANTIAGO	17. El Campeon; the old man
CUBA	18. Santiago's home country
CAMPEON	19. The old man: El ___
DIMAGGIO	20. Baseball great

The Old Man and The Sea Fill In The Blanks 2

_____

1. Santiago's muscular problem with his hands
2. Ocean
3. It holds a sail.
4. The fish's splash got Santiago all ____.
5. The fish are our ____.
6. They attacked and ate the big fish.
7. Santiago got his nickname from arm ____ in his youth.
8. Fish lure
9. Daily news publication
10. Large hook with which one pulls in a lined fish
11. Tied rope-like things that catch fish
12. Santiago ate ____ fish from the bigger fish's stomach.
13. Santiago hit the sharks with one.
14. El Campeon; the old man
15. Pub/restaurant owner
16. Kind of tuna
17. Santiago's home country
18. Leftover bones
19. The worst kind of bad luck
20. Baseball club

The Old Man and The Sea Fill In The Blanks 2 Answer Key

CRAMPS	1. Santiago's muscular problem with his hands
SEA	2. Ocean
MAST	3. It holds a sail.
WET	4. The fish's splash got Santiago all ____.
BROTHERS	5. The fish are our ____.
SHARKS	6. They attacked and ate the big fish.
WRESTLING	7. Santiago got his nickname from arm ____ in his youth.
BAIT	8. Fish lure
NEWSPAPER	9. Daily news publication
GAFF	10. Large hook with which one pulls in a lined fish
NETS	11. Tied rope-like things that catch fish
FLYING	12. Santiago ate ____ fish from the bigger fish's stomach.
CLUB	13. Santiago hit the sharks with one.
SANTIAGO	14. El Campeon; the old man
MARTIN	15. Pub/restaurant owner
BONITO	16. Kind of tuna
CUBA	17. Santiago's home country
CARCASS	18. Leftover bones
SALAO	19. The worst kind of bad luck
BAT	20. Baseball club

Copyrighted

The Old Man and The Sea Fill In The Blanks 3

_____

1. Daily news publication
2. The old man: El ___
3. El Campeon; the old man
4. The fish's splash got Santiago all ____.
5. Santiago had a streak of bad ____
6. It holds a sail.
7. Yellow ____; a friendly, wishful joke
8. Santiago hit the sharks with one.
9. Large hook with which one pulls in a lined fish
10. Second kind of fish Santiago ate
11. The boy
12. Loss
13. The worst kind of bad luck
14. The fish are our ____.
15. Santiago's muscular problem with his hands
16. Santiago tied his knife to one to make a weapon.
17. Kind of fish the old man caught
18. Baseball club
19. Santiago ate ____ fish from the bigger fish's stomach.
20. Fish lure

The Old Man and The Sea Fill In The Blanks 3 Answer Key

NEWSPAPER	1. Daily news publication
CAMPEON	2. The old man: El ___
SANTIAGO	3. El Campeon; the old man
WET	4. The fish's splash got Santiago all ____.
LUCK	5. Santiago had a streak of bad ____
MAST	6. It holds a sail.
RICE	7. Yellow ____; a friendly, wishful joke
CLUB	8. Santiago hit the sharks with one.
GAFF	9. Large hook with which one pulls in a lined fish
DOLPHIN	10. Second kind of fish Santiago ate
MANOLIN	11. The boy
DEFEAT	12. Loss
SALAO	13. The worst kind of bad luck
BROTHERS	14. The fish are our ____.
CRAMPS	15. Santiago's muscular problem with his hands
OAR	16. Santiago tied his knife to one to make a weapon.
MARLIN	17. Kind of fish the old man caught
BAT	18. Baseball club
FLYING	19. Santiago ate ____ fish from the bigger fish's stomach.
BAIT	20. Fish lure

The Old Man and The Sea Fill In The Blanks 4

1. The boy
2. What the big fish did to Santiago's boat
3. It is better to be lucky. But I would rather be ____
4. Ocean
5. Baseball great
6. Large hook with which one pulls in a lined fish
7. Second kind of fish Santiago ate
8. El Campeon; the old man
9. Loss
10. Subject of the old man's dreams
11. Santiago had a streak of bad ____
12. Kind of fish the old man caught
13. Fish lure
14. Leftover bones
15. They attacked and ate the big fish.
16. The worst kind of bad luck
17. Santiago's muscular problem with his hands
18. Santiago got a cut below his ____ when the fish pulled him over.
19. Tied rope-like things that catch fish
20. Small house, usually run-down

The Old Man and The Sea Fill In The Blanks 4 Answer Key

MANOLIN	1. The boy
TOWED	2. What the big fish did to Santiago's boat
EXACT	3. It is better to be lucky. But I would rather be ____
SEA	4. Ocean
DIMAGGIO	5. Baseball great
GAFF	6. Large hook with which one pulls in a lined fish
DOLPHIN	7. Second kind of fish Santiago ate
SANTIAGO	8. El Campeon; the old man
DEFEAT	9. Loss
LIONS	10. Subject of the old man's dreams
LUCK	11. Santiago had a streak of bad ____
MARLIN	12. Kind of fish the old man caught
BAIT	13. Fish lure
CARCASS	14. Leftover bones
SHARKS	15. They attacked and ate the big fish.
SALAO	16. The worst kind of bad luck
CRAMPS	17. Santiago's muscular problem with his hands
EYE	18. Santiago got a cut below his ____ when the fish pulled him over.
NETS	19. Tied rope-like things that catch fish
SHACK	20. Small house, usually run-down

The Old Man and The Sea Matching 1

___ 1. TRICKS   A. Second kind of fish Santiago ate
___ 2. BAIT   B. Santiago tied his knife to one to make a weapon.
___ 3. EXACT   C. Baseball great
___ 4. TOWED   D. Santiago hit the sharks with one.
___ 5. NETS   E. It is better to be lucky. But I would rather be ____
___ 6. MAST   F. He received the head of the fish from Santiago
___ 7. WET   G. It holds a sail.
___ 8. CLUB   H. Ocean
___ 9. CRAMPS   I. I know many ____ and I have resolution.
___10. SHACK   J. Yellow ____; a friendly, wishful joke
___11. OAR   K. Fish lure
___12. DIMAGGIO   L. Pub/restaurant owner
___13. FLYING   M. Santiago ate ____ fish from the bigger fish's stomach.
___14. BAT   N. Subject of the old man's dreams
___15. SEA   O. Small house, usually run-down
___16. SHARKS   P. The fish's splash got Santiago all ____.
___17. LIONS   Q. Santiago had a streak of bad ____
___18. RICE   R. Leftover bones
___19. DOLPHIN   S. El Campeon; the old man
___20. MARTIN   T. Tied rope-like things that catch fish
___21. LUCK   U. They attacked and ate the big fish.
___22. BROTHERS   V. What the big fish did to Santiago's boat
___23. SANTIAGO   W. The fish are our ____.
___24. PEDRICO   X. Baseball club
___25. CARCASS   Y. Santiago's muscular problem with his hands

The Old Man and The Sea Matching 1 Answer Key

I - 1. TRICKS	A.	Second kind of fish Santiago ate
K - 2. BAIT	B.	Santiago tied his knife to one to make a weapon.
E - 3. EXACT	C.	Baseball great
V - 4. TOWED	D.	Santiago hit the sharks with one.
T - 5. NETS	E.	It is better to be lucky. But I would rather be ____
G - 6. MAST	F.	He received the head of the fish from Santiago
P - 7. WET	G.	It holds a sail.
D - 8. CLUB	H.	Ocean
Y - 9. CRAMPS	I.	I know many ____ and I have resolution.
O -10. SHACK	J.	Yellow ____; a friendly, wishful joke
B -11. OAR	K.	Fish lure
C -12. DIMAGGIO	L.	Pub/restaurant owner
M -13. FLYING	M.	Santiago ate ____ fish from the bigger fish's stomach.
X -14. BAT	N.	Subject of the old man's dreams
H -15. SEA	O.	Small house, usually run-down
U -16. SHARKS	P.	The fish's splash got Santiago all ____.
N -17. LIONS	Q.	Santiago had a streak of bad ____
J -18. RICE	R.	Leftover bones
A -19. DOLPHIN	S.	El Campeon; the old man
L -20. MARTIN	T.	Tied rope-like things that catch fish
Q -21. LUCK	U.	They attacked and ate the big fish.
W -22. BROTHERS	V.	What the big fish did to Santiago's boat
S -23. SANTIAGO	W.	The fish are our ____.
F -24. PEDRICO	X.	Baseball club
R -25. CARCASS	Y.	Santiago's muscular problem with his hands

Copyrighted

The Old Man and The Sea Matching 2

___ 1. SKIFF   A. Fish lure
___ 2. DEFEAT   B. It holds a sail.
___ 3. DOLPHIN   C. Santiago tied his knife to one to make a weapon.
___ 4. TRICKS   D. Sharp instrument that finally killed the big fish
___ 5. CAMPEON   E. Yellow ____; a friendly, wishful joke
___ 6. HARPOON   F. Loss
___ 7. RICE   G. Kind of fish the old man caught
___ 8. MARLIN   H. I know many ____ and I have resolution.
___ 9. WRESTLING   I. The old man: El ___
___10. BAIT   J. Ocean
___11. BAT   K. Subject of the old man's dreams
___12. SEA   L. Pub/restaurant owner
___13. FLYING   M. Santiago got his nickname from arm ____ in his youth.
___14. MAST   N. Tied rope-like things that catch fish
___15. WET   O. They attacked and ate the big fish.
___16. OAR   P. The fish's splash got Santiago all ____.
___17. LIONS   Q. The fish are our ____.
___18. EXACT   R. Second kind of fish Santiago ate
___19. MARTIN   S. Baseball club
___20. BROTHERS   T. Santiago hit the sharks with one.
___21. PEDRICO   U. It is better to be lucky. But I would rather be ____
___22. NETS   V. He received the head of the fish from Santiago
___23. CLUB   W. Santiago got a cut below his ____ when the fish pulled him over.
___24. SHARKS   X. Santiago's kind of boat
___25. EYE   Y. Santiago ate ____ fish from the bigger fish's stomach.

The Old Man and The Sea Matching 2 Answer Key

X - 1. SKIFF	A. Fish lure
F - 2. DEFEAT	B. It holds a sail.
R - 3. DOLPHIN	C. Santiago tied his knife to one to make a weapon.
H - 4. TRICKS	D. Sharp instrument that finally killed the big fish
I - 5. CAMPEON	E. Yellow ____; a friendly, wishful joke
D - 6. HARPOON	F. Loss
E - 7. RICE	G. Kind of fish the old man caught
G - 8. MARLIN	H. I know many ____ and I have resolution.
M - 9. WRESTLING	I. The old man: El ___
A - 10. BAIT	J. Ocean
S - 11. BAT	K. Subject of the old man's dreams
J - 12. SEA	L. Pub/restaurant owner
Y - 13. FLYING	M. Santiago got his nickname from arm ____ in his youth.
B - 14. MAST	N. Tied rope-like things that catch fish
P - 15. WET	O. They attacked and ate the big fish.
C - 16. OAR	P. The fish's splash got Santiago all ____.
K - 17. LIONS	Q. The fish are our ____.
U - 18. EXACT	R. Second kind of fish Santiago ate
L - 19. MARTIN	S. Baseball club
Q - 20. BROTHERS	T. Santiago hit the sharks with one.
V - 21. PEDRICO	U. It is better to be lucky. But I would rather be ____
N - 22. NETS	V. He received the head of the fish from Santiago
T - 23. CLUB	W. Santiago got a cut below his ____ when the fish pulled him over.
O - 24. SHARKS	X. Santiago's kind of boat
W - 25. EYE	Y. Santiago ate ____ fish from the bigger fish's stomach.

The Old Man and The Sea Matching 3

___ 1. DEFEAT   A. Santiago's kind of boat
___ 2. MANOLIN   B. Santiago's muscular problem with his hands
___ 3. LUCK   C. It holds a sail.
___ 4. BAIT   D. Large hook with which one pulls in a lined fish
___ 5. CUBA   E. Santiago tied his knife to one to make a weapon.
___ 6. SALAO   F. I know many ____ and I have resolution.
___ 7. GAFF   G. Loss
___ 8. PEDRICO   H. Santiago's home country
___ 9. SKIFF   I. Pub/restaurant owner
___10. MAST   J. He received the head of the fish from Santiago
___11. CARCASS   K. Tied rope-like things that catch fish
___12. TRICKS   L. Santiago had a streak of bad ____
___13. SHARKS   M. Kind of tuna
___14. BROTHERS   N. They attacked and ate the big fish.
___15. EXACT   O. Santiago got a cut below his ____ when the fish pulled him over.
___16. HARPOON   P. The worst kind of bad luck
___17. BONITO   Q. Sharp instrument that finally killed the big fish
___18. MARTIN   R. The fish are our ____.
___19. EYE   S. Leftover bones
___20. NETS   T. The boy
___21. SANTIAGO   U. It is better to be lucky. But I would rather be ____
___22. OAR   V. Kind of fish the old man caught
___23. MARLIN   W. What the big fish did to Santiago's boat
___24. TOWED   X. El Campeon; the old man
___25. CRAMPS   Y. Fish lure

The Old Man and The Sea Matching 3 Answer Key

G - 1. DEFEAT
T - 2. MANOLIN
L - 3. LUCK
Y - 4. BAIT
H - 5. CUBA
P - 6. SALAO
D - 7. GAFF
J - 8. PEDRICO
A - 9. SKIFF
C - 10. MAST
S - 11. CARCASS
F - 12. TRICKS
N - 13. SHARKS
R - 14. BROTHERS
U - 15. EXACT
Q - 16. HARPOON
M - 17. BONITO
I - 18. MARTIN
O - 19. EYE
K - 20. NETS
X - 21. SANTIAGO
E - 22. OAR
V - 23. MARLIN
W - 24. TOWED
B - 25. CRAMPS

A. Santiago's kind of boat
B. Santiago's muscular problem with his hands
C. It holds a sail.
D. Large hook with which one pulls in a lined fish
E. Santiago tied his knife to one to make a weapon.
F. I know many ____ and I have resolution.
G. Loss
H. Santiago's home country
I. Pub/restaurant owner
J. He received the head of the fish from Santiago
K. Tied rope-like things that catch fish
L. Santiago had a streak of bad ____
M. Kind of tuna
N. They attacked and ate the big fish.
O. Santiago got a cut below his ____ when the fish pulled him over.
P. The worst kind of bad luck
Q. Sharp instrument that finally killed the big fish
R. The fish are our ____.
S. Leftover bones
T. The boy
U. It is better to be lucky. But I would rather be ____
V. Kind of fish the old man caught
W. What the big fish did to Santiago's boat
X. El Campeon; the old man
Y. Fish lure

The Old Man and The Sea Matching 4

___ 1. CUBA   A. Subject of the old man's dreams
___ 2. MAST   B. Yellow ____; a friendly, wishful joke
___ 3. HARPOON   C. The fish are our ____.
___ 4. BROTHERS   D. The old man: El ___
___ 5. SEA   E. I know many ____ and I have resolution.
___ 6. SALAO   F. Small house, usually run-down
___ 7. RICE   G. Santiago got a cut below his ____ when the fish pulled him over.
___ 8. MARTIN   H. Daily news publication
___ 9. SANTIAGO   I. Sharp instrument that finally killed the big fish
___10. NEWSPAPER   J. Santiago's home country
___11. NETS   K. It holds a sail.
___12. BAT   L. Baseball club
___13. GAFF   M. The fish's splash got Santiago all ____.
___14. DIMAGGIO   N. Ocean
___15. WRESTLING   O. The boy
___16. EYE   P. Kind of tuna
___17. SHARKS   Q. Pub/restaurant owner
___18. SHACK   R. Baseball great
___19. BONITO   S. Large hook with which one pulls in a lined fish
___20. LIONS   T. The worst kind of bad luck
___21. CARCASS   U. Tied rope-like things that catch fish
___22. CAMPEON   V. El Campeon; the old man
___23. MANOLIN   W. Santiago got his nickname from arm____ in his youth.
___24. TRICKS   X. They attacked and ate the big fish.
___25. WET   Y. Leftover bones

The Old Man and The Sea Matching 4 Answer Key

J - 1. CUBA   A. Subject of the old man's dreams
K - 2. MAST   B. Yellow ____; a friendly, wishful joke
I - 3. HARPOON   C. The fish are our ____.
C - 4. BROTHERS   D. The old man: El ___
N - 5. SEA   E. I know many ____ and I have resolution.
T - 6. SALAO   F. Small house, usually run-down
B - 7. RICE   G. Santiago got a cut below his ____ when the fish pulled him over.
Q - 8. MARTIN   H. Daily news publication
V - 9. SANTIAGO   I. Sharp instrument that finally killed the big fish
H -10. NEWSPAPER   J. Santiago's home country
U -11. NETS   K. It holds a sail.
L -12. BAT   L. Baseball club
S -13. GAFF   M. The fish's splash got Santiago all ____.
R -14. DIMAGGIO   N. Ocean
W -15. WRESTLING   O. The boy
G -16. EYE   P. Kind of tuna
X -17. SHARKS   Q. Pub/restaurant owner
F -18. SHACK   R. Baseball great
P -19. BONITO   S. Large hook with which one pulls in a lined fish
A -20. LIONS   T. The worst kind of bad luck
Y -21. CARCASS   U. Tied rope-like things that catch fish
D -22. CAMPEON   V. El Campeon; the old man
O -23. MANOLIN   W. Santiago got his nickname from arm ____ in his youth.
E -24. TRICKS   X. They attacked and ate the big fish.
M -25. WET   Y. Leftover bones

The Old Man and The Sea Magic Squares 1

Match the definition with the vocabulary word. Put your answers in the magic squares below. When your answers are correct, all columns and rows will add to the same number.

A. WRESTLING
B. BAIT
C. OAR
D. SALAO
E. PEDRICO
F. MARTIN
G. DOLPHIN
H. BROTHERS
I. CAMPEON
J. CLUB
K. LIONS
L. FLYING
M. RICE
N. GAFF
O. TRICKS
P. MANOLIN

1. Large hook with which one pulls in a lined fish
2. Second kind of fish Santiago ate
3. Santiago ate ____ fish from the bigger fish's stomach.
4. Santiago got his nickname from arm ____ in his youth.
5. Subject of the old man's dreams
6. Fish lure
7. Yellow ____; a friendly, wishful joke
8. The fish are our ____.
9. He received the head of the fish from Santiago
10. The boy
11. Santiago tied his knife to one to make a weapon.
12. Santiago hit the sharks with one.
13. The worst kind of bad luck
14. The old man: El ___
15. Pub/restaurant owner
16. I know man___ and I have resolution.

A=	B=	C=	D=
E=	F=	G=	H=
I=	J=	K=	L=
M=	N=	O=	P=

The Old Man and The Sea Magic Squares 1 Answer Key

Match the definition with the vocabulary word. Put your answers in the magic squares below. When your answers are correct, all columns and rows will add to the same number.

A. WRESTLING
B. BAIT
C. OAR
D. SALAO
E. PEDRICO
F. MARTIN
G. DOLPHIN
H. BROTHERS
I. CAMPEON
J. CLUB
K. LIONS
L. FLYING
M. RICE
N. GAFF
O. TRICKS
P. MANOLIN

1. Large hook with which one pulls in a lined fish
2. Second kind of fish Santiago ate
3. Santiago ate ____ fish from the bigger fish's stomach.
4. Santiago got his nickname from arm ____ in his youth.
5. Subject of the old man's dreams
6. Fish lure
7. Yellow ____; a friendly, wishful joke
8. The fish are our ____.
9. He received the head of the fish from Santiago
10. The boy
11. Santiago tied his knife to one to make a weapon.
12. Santiago hit the sharks with one.
13. The worst kind of bad luck
14. The old man: El ____
15. Pub/restaurant owner
16. I know man____ and I have resolution.

A=4	B=6	C=11	D=13
E=9	F=15	G=2	H=8
I=14	J=12	K=5	L=3
M=7	N=1	O=16	P=10

The Old Man and The Sea Magic Squares 2

Match the definition with the vocabulary word. Put your answers in the magic squares below. When your answers are correct, all columns and rows will add to the same number.

A. SHARKS
B. LIONS
C. NEWSPAPER
D. MANOLIN
E. SANTIAGO
F. WET
G. DOLPHIN
H. DEFEAT
I. CRAMPS
J. SEA
K. PEDRICO
L. SHACK
M. OAR
N. BAT
O. BROTHERS
P. CARCASS

1. Loss
2. Santiago tied his knife to one to make a weapon.
3. Subject of the old man's dreams
4. He received the head of the fish from Santiago
5. Ocean
6. Daily news publication
7. Leftover bones
8. El Campeon; the old man
9. The fish are our ____.
10. The fish's splash got Santiago all ____.
11. Santiago's muscular problem with his hands
12. The boy
13. They attacked and ate the big fish.
14. Small house, usually run-down
15. Second kind of fish Santiago ate
16. Baseball club

A=	B=	C=	D=
E=	F=	G=	H=
I=	J=	K=	L=
M=	N=	O=	P=

The Old Man and The Sea Magic Squares 2 Answer Key

Match the definition with the vocabulary word. Put your answers in the magic squares below. When your answers are correct, all columns and rows will add to the same number.

A. SHARKS
B. LIONS
C. NEWSPAPER
D. MANOLIN
E. SANTIAGO
F. WET
G. DOLPHIN
H. DEFEAT
I. CRAMPS
J. SEA
K. PEDRICO
L. SHACK
M. OAR
N. BAT
O. BROTHERS
P. CARCASS

1. Loss
2. Santiago tied his knife to one to make a weapon.
3. Subject of the old man's dreams
4. He received the head of the fish from Santiago
5. Ocean
6. Daily news publication
7. Leftover bones
8. El Campeon; the old man
9. The fish are our ____.
10. The fish's splash got Santiago all ____.
11. Santiago's muscular problem with his hands
12. The boy
13. They attacked and ate the big fish.
14. Small house, usually run-down
15. Second kind of fish Santiago ate
16. Baseball club

A=13	B=3	C=6	D=12
E=8	F=10	G=15	H=1
I=11	J=5	K=4	L=14
M=2	N=16	O=9	P=7

The Old Man and The Sea Magic Squares 3

Match the definition with the vocabulary word. Put your answers in the magic squares below. When your answers are correct, all columns and rows will add to the same number.

A. CLUB
B. FLYING
C. GAFF
D. CRAMPS
E. PEDRICO
F. BROTHERS
G. SHACK
H. DEFEAT
I. HARPOON
J. RICE
K. SEA
L. MANOLIN
M. TRICKS
N. MAST
O. LIONS
P. SANTIAGO

1. Santiago ate ____ fish from the bigger fish's stomach.
2. Small house, usually run-down
3. Ocean
4. It holds a sail.
5. I know many ____ and I have resolution.
6. The boy
7. Loss
8. Santiago hit the sharks with one.
9. El Campeon; the old man
10. Sharp instrument that finally killed the big fish
11. He received the head of the fish from Santiago
12. Santiago's muscular problem with his hands
13. Large hook with which one pulls in a lined fish
14. The fish are our ____.
15. Yellow ____; a friendly, wishful joke
16. Subject of the old man's dreams

A=	B=	C=	D=
E=	F=	G=	H=
I=	J=	K=	L=
M=	N=	O=	P=

The Old Man and The Sea Magic Squares 3 Answer Key

Match the definition with the vocabulary word. Put your answers in the magic squares below. When your answers are correct, all columns and rows will add to the same number.

A. CLUB
B. FLYING
C. GAFF
D. CRAMPS
E. PEDRICO
F. BROTHERS
G. SHACK
H. DEFEAT
I. HARPOON
J. RICE
K. SEA
L. MANOLIN
M. TRICKS
N. MAST
O. LIONS
P. SANTIAGO

1. Santiago ate ____ fish from the bigger fish's stomach.
2. Small house, usually run-down
3. Ocean
4. It holds a sail.
5. I know many ____ and I have resolution.
6. The boy
7. Loss
8. Santiago hit the sharks with one.
9. El Campeon; the old man
10. Sharp instrument that finally killed the big fish
11. He received the head of the fish from Santiago
12. Santiago's muscular problem with his hands
13. Large hook with which one pulls in a lined fish
14. The fish are our ____.
15. Yellow ____; a friendly, wishful joke
16. Subject of the old man's dreams

A=8	B=1	C=13	D=12
E=11	F=14	G=2	H=7
I=10	J=15	K=3	L=6
M=5	N=4	O=16	P=9

The Old Man and The Sea Magic Squares 4

Match the definition with the vocabulary word. Put your answers in the magic squares below. When your answers are correct, all columns and rows will add to the same number.

A. BONITO
B. SHARKS
C. CRAMPS
D. BAT
E. WRESTLING
F. SANTIAGO
G. DIMAGGIO
H. OAR
I. DOLPHIN
J. SHACK
K. MAST
L. SEA
M. NETS
N. MARTIN
O. GAFF
P. CARCASS

1. Santiago tied his knife to one to make a weapon.
2. Kind of tuna
3. They attacked and ate the big fish.
4. Baseball great
5. Small house, usually run-down
6. Large hook with which one pulls in a lined fish
7. Leftover bones
8. Second kind of fish Santiago ate
9. It holds a sail.
10. Pub/restaurant owner
11. Tied rope-like things that catch fish
12. Ocean
13. Santiago got his nickname from arm ____ in his youth.
14. Baseball club
15. Santiago's muscular problem with his hands
16. El Campeon; the old man

A=	B=	C=	D=
E=	F=	G=	H=
I=	J=	K=	L=
M=	N=	O=	P=

The Old Man and The Sea Magic Squares 4 Answer Key

Match the definition with the vocabulary word. Put your answers in the magic squares below. When your answers are correct, all columns and rows will add to the same number.

A. BONITO
B. SHARKS
C. CRAMPS
D. BAT
E. WRESTLING
F. SANTIAGO
G. DIMAGGIO
H. OAR
I. DOLPHIN
J. SHACK
K. MAST
L. SEA
M. NETS
N. MARTIN
O. GAFF
P. CARCASS

1. Santiago tied his knife to one to make a weapon.
2. Kind of tuna
3. They attacked and ate the big fish.
4. Baseball great
5. Small house, usually run-down
6. Large hook with which one pulls in a lined fish
7. Leftover bones
8. Second kind of fish Santiago ate
9. It holds a sail.
10. Pub/restaurant owner
11. Tied rope-like things that catch fish
12. Ocean
13. Santiago got his nickname from arm ____ in his youth.
14. Baseball club
15. Santiago's muscular problem with his hands
16. El Campeon; the old man

A=2	B=3	C=15	D=14
E=13	F=16	G=4	H=1
I=8	J=5	K=9	L=12
M=11	N=10	O=6	P=7

The Old Man and The Sea Word Search 1

```
P Y C J K F L K M G W N F S M Y D G J B
X T A R F B V H J D K Y F Q P C C N W S
Q X R K Q O N F T T C C K M Q J S I L M
V L C F R N K G L O N J G V F K L B F
Y W A L P I M G K W L Q A P T E I T B T
T X S T I T N A H E S W F M I Y F S A P
Y J S B W O C I R D E P F T A E F E D M
B A F H E P N A E L B S R L B N S R D T
M T F P A K O S P T I I S S Y C O W V N
T Q M M K R D H A B C N A G Q I S L O L
V A S N J I K B P K L B N Y N T N O I K
C J A X F C G S S D R R T D E D P G B N
S M L J P E T H W I T O I N O R Y H P K
E X A C T E W M E M Q T A Y A L S K M D
S K O R F L L S N A B H G H W Y P D L Z
C N T Y T W H H V G V E O R F F M H X P
X L Q M W I D A D G N R R P C F A M I C
K C U L D C N C T I L S C U B A R Y X N
T F D B X J R K D O H G Z H K P C D C D
```

Baseball club (3)
Baseball great (8)
Daily news publication (9)
El Campeon; the old man (8)
Fish lure (4)
He received the head of the fish from Santiago (7)
I know many ____ and I have resolution. (6)
It holds a sail. (4)
It is better to be lucky. But I would rather be ____ (5)
Kind of fish the old man caught (6)
Kind of tuna (6)
Large hook with which one pulls in a lined fish (4)
Leftover bones (7)
Loss (6)
Ocean (3)
Pub/restaurant owner (6)
Santiago ate ____ fish from the bigger fish's stomach. (6)
Santiago got a cut below his ____ when the fish pulled him over. (3)
Santiago got his nickname from arm ____ in his youth. (9)

Santiago had a streak of bad ____ (4)
Santiago hit the sharks with one. (4)
Santiago tied his knife to one to make a weapon. (3)
Santiago's home country (4)
Santiago's kind of boat (5)
Santiago's muscular problem with his hands (6)
Second kind of fish Santiago ate (7)
Sharp instrument that finally killed the big fish (7)
Small house, usually run-down (5)
Subject of the old man's dreams (5)
The boy (7)
The fish are our ____. (8)
The fish's splash got Santiago all ____. (3)
The old man: El ____ (7)
The worst kind of bad luck (5)
They attacked and ate the big fish. (6)
Tied rope-like things that catch fish (4)
What the big fish did to Santiago's boat (5)
Yellow ____; a friendly, wishful joke (4)

The Old Man and The Sea Word Search 1 Answer Key

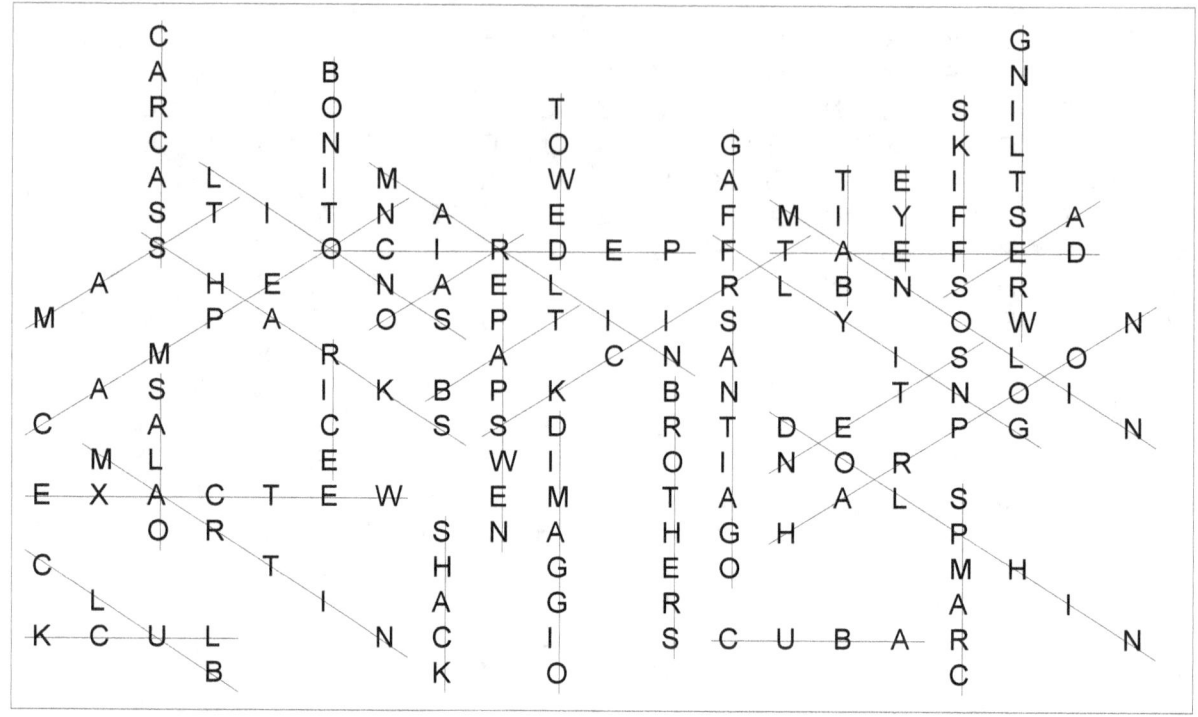

Baseball club (3)
Baseball great (8)
Daily news publication (9)
El Campeon; the old man (8)
Fish lure (4)
He received the head of the fish from Santiago (7)
I know many ____ and I have resolution. (6)
It holds a sail. (4)
It is better to be lucky. But I would rather be ____ (5)
Kind of fish the old man caught (6)
Kind of tuna (6)
Large hook with which one pulls in a lined fish (4)
Leftover bones (7)
Loss (6)
Ocean (3)
Pub/restaurant owner (6)
Santiago ate ____ fish from the bigger fish's stomach. (6)
Santiago got a cut below his ____ when the fish pulled him over. (3)
Santiago got his nickname from arm ____ in his youth. (9)
Santiago had a streak of bad ____ (4)
Santiago hit the sharks with one. (4)
Santiago tied his knife to one to make a weapon. (3)
Santiago's home country (4)
Santiago's kind of boat (5)
Santiago's muscular problem with his hands (6)
Second kind of fish Santiago ate (7)
Sharp instrument that finally killed the big fish (7)
Small house, usually run-down (5)
Subject of the old man's dreams (5)
The boy (7)
The fish are our ____. (8)
The fish's splash got Santiago all ____. (3)
The old man: El ____ (7)
The worst kind of bad luck (5)
They attacked and ate the big fish. (6)
Tied rope-like things that catch fish (4)
What the big fish did to Santiago's boat (5)
Yellow ____; a friendly, wishful joke (4)

The Old Man and The Sea Word Search 2

```
T H B R C T V J D Y G F Y F R Q J K Q S
F Q C G V V N T Z Y H W K S G O A L A S
Z W S K C I C Z S P Z P C B P E B J R A
D L K F L C C A G C V N A A S K Y E O C
O M A R T I N O O P R A H T R G H C C R
L A A N Q T O E V M J R S P N T I U L A
P M R R I H E L W L W V B I O R P B U C
H N P A M B P R Y S P N Y R D F H A B M
I D G L V Q M P S B P L B E S B A I T M
N O G D M S A X G Q F A P C P H V V E H
M B S S K M C R E S K M P L M L A L W D
K D T C X W D K Z Y R A N E A B U R B X
G N I L T S E R W F E N P G R J S C K F
O R C M Z X F W H R L O D A C K N D K S
T G P B A L K H X D Y L S F I M E E T Y
I W S C R G P X E F K I Y F B A T F H Z
N N T Q I W G W M D M N F F X S S E D C
O F M Z C R O I D B J X K Q V T Q A Z W
B X F F E T K B O L I O N S J L N T S J
```

Baseball club (3)
Baseball great (8)
Daily news publication (9)
El Campeon; the old man (8)
Fish lure (4)
He received the head of the fish from Santiago (7)
I know many ____ and I have resolution. (6)
It holds a sail. (4)
It is better to be lucky. But I would rather be ____ (5)
Kind of fish the old man caught (6)
Kind of tuna (6)
Large hook with which one pulls in a lined fish (4)
Leftover bones (7)
Loss (6)
Ocean (3)
Pub/restaurant owner (6)
Santiago ate ____ fish from the bigger fish's stomach. (6)
Santiago got a cut below his ____ when the fish pulled him over. (3)
Santiago got his nickname from arm ____ in his youth. (9)

Santiago had a streak of bad ____(4)
Santiago hit the sharks with one. (4)
Santiago tied his knife to one to make a weapon. (3)
Santiago's home country (4)
Santiago's kind of boat (5)
Santiago's muscular problem with his hands (6)
Second kind of fish Santiago ate (7)
Sharp instrument that finally killed the big fish (7)
Small house, usually run-down (5)
Subject of the old man's dreams (5)
The boy (7)
The fish are our ____. (8)
The fish's splash got Santiago all ____. (3)
The old man: El ____ (7)
The worst kind of bad luck (5)
They attacked and ate the big fish. (6)
Tied rope-like things that catch fish (4)
What the big fish did to Santiago's boat (5)
Yellow ____; a friendly, wishful joke (4)

The Old Man and The Sea Word Search 2 Answer Key

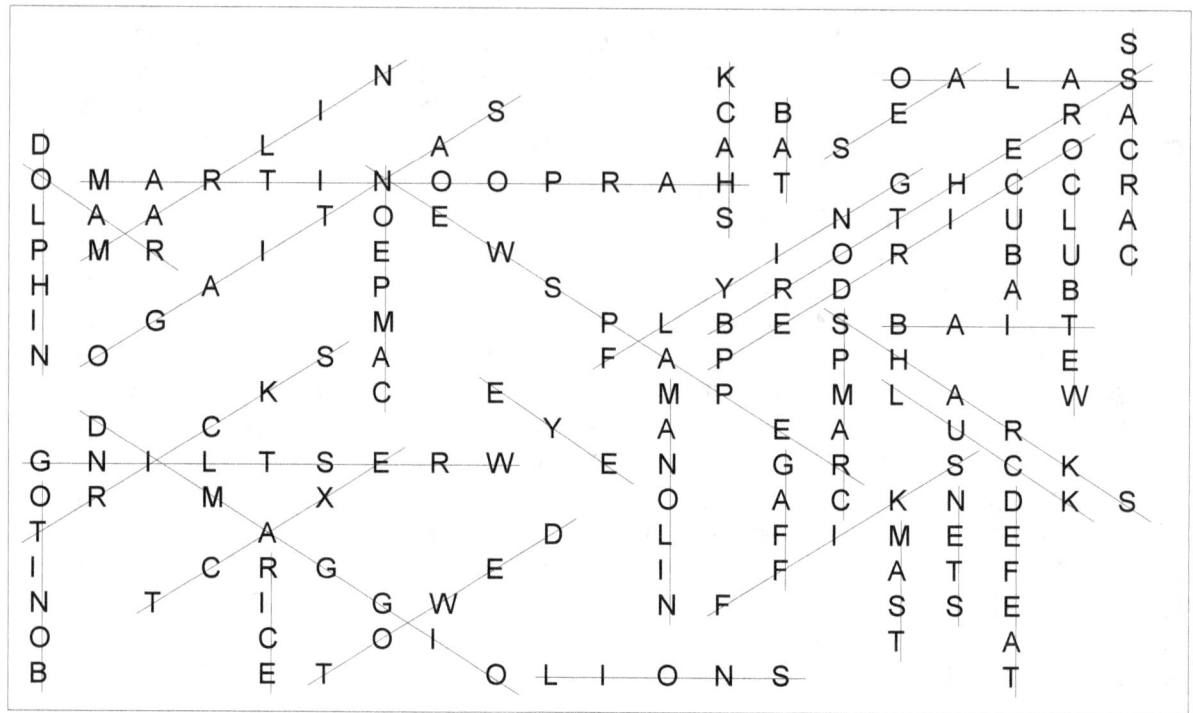

Baseball club (3)
Baseball great (8)
Daily news publication (9)
El Campeon; the old man (8)
Fish lure (4)
He received the head of the fish from Santiago (7)
I know many ____ and I have resolution. (6)
It holds a sail. (4)
It is better to be lucky. But I would rather be ____ (5)
Kind of fish the old man caught (6)
Kind of tuna (6)
Large hook with which one pulls in a lined fish (4)
Leftover bones (7)
Loss (6)
Ocean (3)
Pub/restaurant owner (6)
Santiago ate ____ fish from the bigger fish's stomach. (6)
Santiago got a cut below his ____ when the fish pulled him over. (3)
Santiago got his nickname from arm ____ in his youth. (9)

Santiago had a streak of bad ____ (4)
Santiago hit the sharks with one. (4)
Santiago tied his knife to one to make a weapon. (3)
Santiago's home country (4)
Santiago's kind of boat (5)
Santiago's muscular problem with his hands (6)
Second kind of fish Santiago ate (7)
Sharp instrument that finally killed the big fish (7)
Small house, usually run-down (5)
Subject of the old man's dreams (5)
The boy (7)
The fish are our ____. (8)
The fish's splash got Santiago all ____. (3)
The old man: El ____ (7)
The worst kind of bad luck (5)
They attacked and ate the big fish. (6)
Tied rope-like things that catch fish (4)
What the big fish did to Santiago's boat (5)
Yellow ____; a friendly, wishful joke (4)

The Old Man and The Sea Word Search 3

```
C L U B P H P G A F F M M L S J W Q J C
X T C Q R P L H X L W B S A U H W E P R
M B P S C E S S S M S Y D L R C A W T R
J K D C S D N W N M S E Q M G T K R H F
Z C P P R R Y M V G F N C B N R I C K S
G N N G E I O A G E N I T A Z K I N E S
N V L E H C A S A T T L X L M S K C Y A
B O N I T O R T I A B R E P A P S W E N
E D B G O S D G P B B A I B W A E S C C
X M O S R N D G B U M M W C L R S O G C
A R K L B P S G D C A L S A K N H C N P
C R A M P S F L Y I N G O T B S A A S Y
T X G C L H S B S K O N S O A F C R K G
T D X R H G I R V P L W P W T J K C I B
J R Q P M V X N T R I P W E T Z V A F J
S A N T I A G O J X N R R D T Y D S F M
N G G H D Z K S M H A R P O O N K S W P
F W Z K S F X H B W R E S T L I N G Z V
V B S R N R R N Q S D I M A G G I O W P
```

BAIT	DIMAGGIO	MARLIN	SEA
BAT	DOLPHIN	MARTIN	SHACK
BONITO	EXACT	MAST	SHARKS
BROTHERS	EYE	NETS	SKIFF
CAMPEON	FLYING	NEWSPAPER	TOWED
CARCASS	GAFF	OAR	TRICKS
CLUB	HARPOON	PEDRICO	WET
CRAMPS	LIONS	RICE	WRESTLING
CUBA	LUCK	SALAO	
DEFEAT	MANOLIN	SANTIAGO	

The Old Man and The Sea Word Search 3 Answer Key

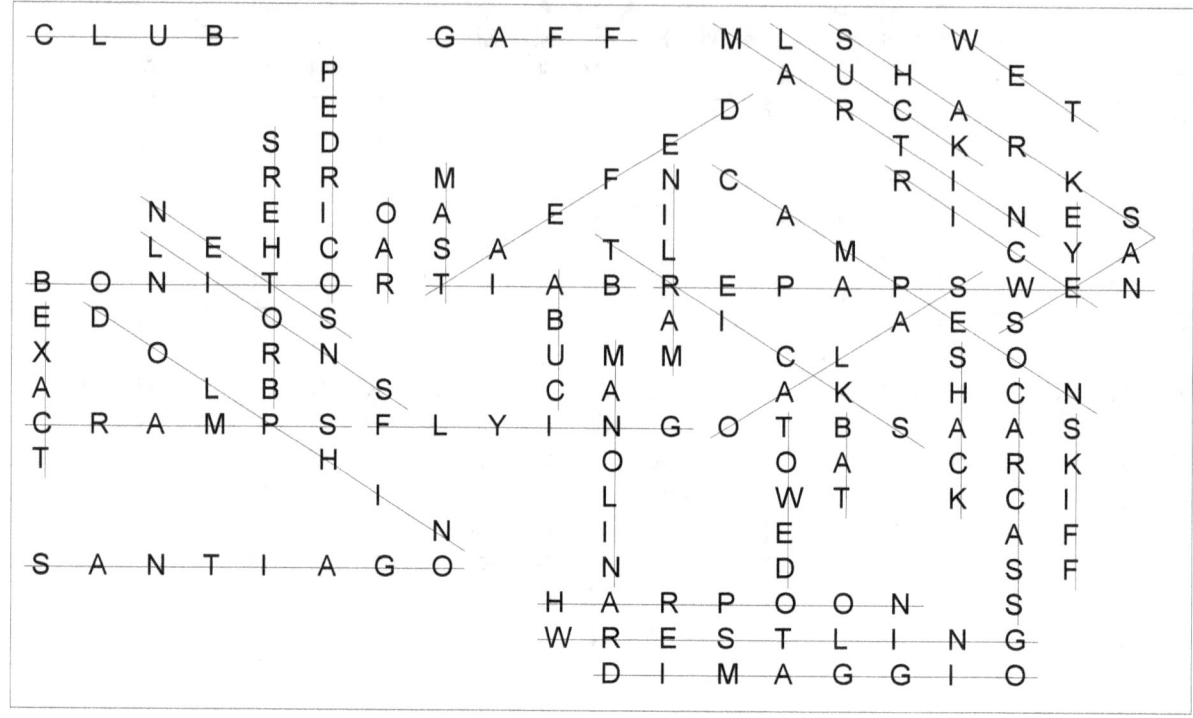

BAIT	DIMAGGIO	MARLIN	SEA
BAT	DOLPHIN	MARTIN	SHACK
BONITO	EXACT	MAST	SHARKS
BROTHERS	EYE	NETS	SKIFF
CAMPEON	FLYING	NEWSPAPER	TOWED
CARCASS	GAFF	OAR	TRICKS
CLUB	HARPOON	PEDRICO	WET
CRAMPS	LIONS	RICE	WRESTLING
CUBA	LUCK	SALAO	
DEFEAT	MANOLIN	SANTIAGO	

The Old Man and The Sea Word Search 4

```
C A R C A S S H A R K S D I M A G G I O
N E W S P A P E R L C L W L H B J C Z C
J Z W W T C T Z J N W W N W V P T S C F
Z S D C J P T H Z M M F Q V T W S J G E
L N A Q S E G T R D S L Y H T L T R Z X
X O Z N P D F E B W C R N P X U D W J A
C I Y C T R C D B L R R A K S C P R E C
X L B O N I T O F E Y E V D S K C I R T
B R U Y R C A F B C S B S P N G I S A R
V H T B Z O A G N A M R M T Q G A F O P
N A X S C G Y T O W I A G H L L J T F K
B R O T H E R S E P R T N N A I A R M Y
L P Q T K A C A P C M D I O M B N P A B
G O L A D F C M M V G H Y M L J Q G R H
T O L E F M W K A R P J L A S I H P T T
T N W F N E T S C L Y M F R W X N D I Z
Q O K E B W Y U O R T H M L H D K Y N D
T N J D N K B D V V D D G I H C K Q Q G
M Q G V N A B S L K K N Q N P M D Q V H
```

BAIT	DIMAGGIO	MARLIN	SEA
BAT	DOLPHIN	MARTIN	SHACK
BONITO	EXACT	MAST	SHARKS
BROTHERS	EYE	NETS	SKIFF
CAMPEON	FLYING	NEWSPAPER	TOWED
CARCASS	GAFF	OAR	TRICKS
CLUB	HARPOON	PEDRICO	WET
CRAMPS	LIONS	RICE	WRESTLING
CUBA	LUCK	SALAO	
DEFEAT	MANOLIN	SANTIAGO	

The Old Man and The Sea Word Search 4 Answer Key

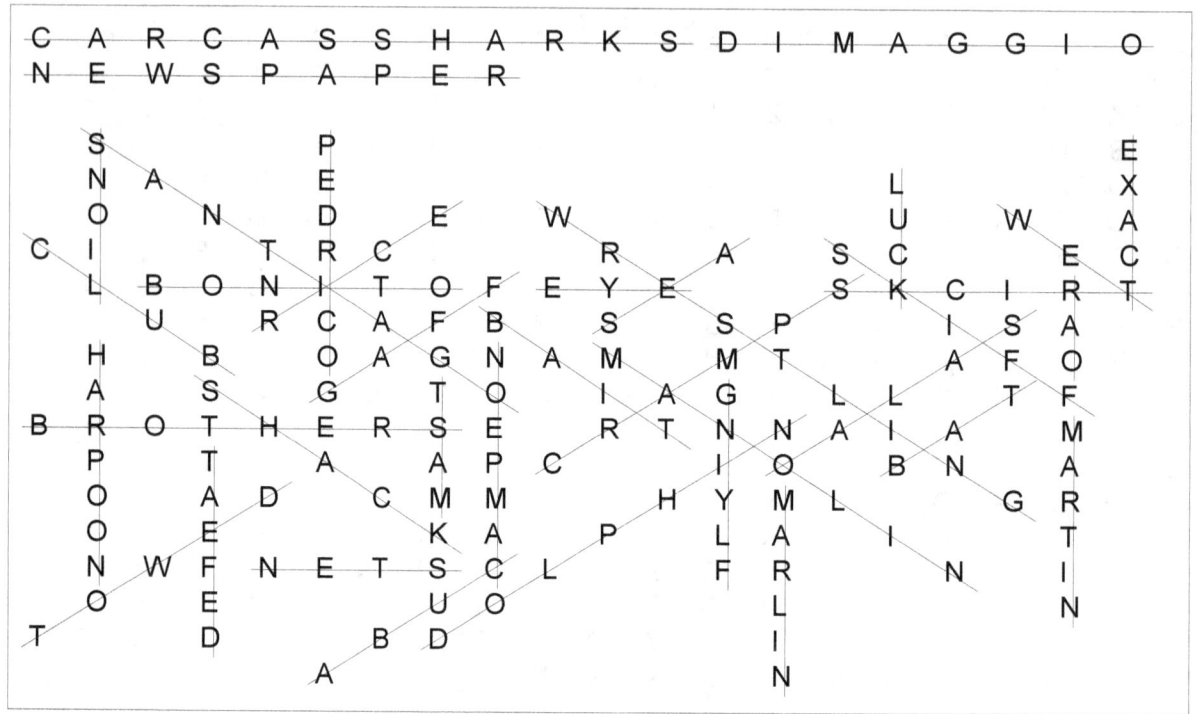

BAIT	DIMAGGIO	MARLIN	SEA
BAT	DOLPHIN	MARTIN	SHACK
BONITO	EXACT	MAST	SHARKS
BROTHERS	EYE	NETS	SKIFF
CAMPEON	FLYING	NEWSPAPER	TOWED
CARCASS	GAFF	OAR	TRICKS
CLUB	HARPOON	PEDRICO	WET
CRAMPS	LIONS	RICE	WRESTLING
CUBA	LUCK	SALAO	
DEFEAT	MANOLIN	SANTIAGO	

The Old Man and The Sea Crossword 1

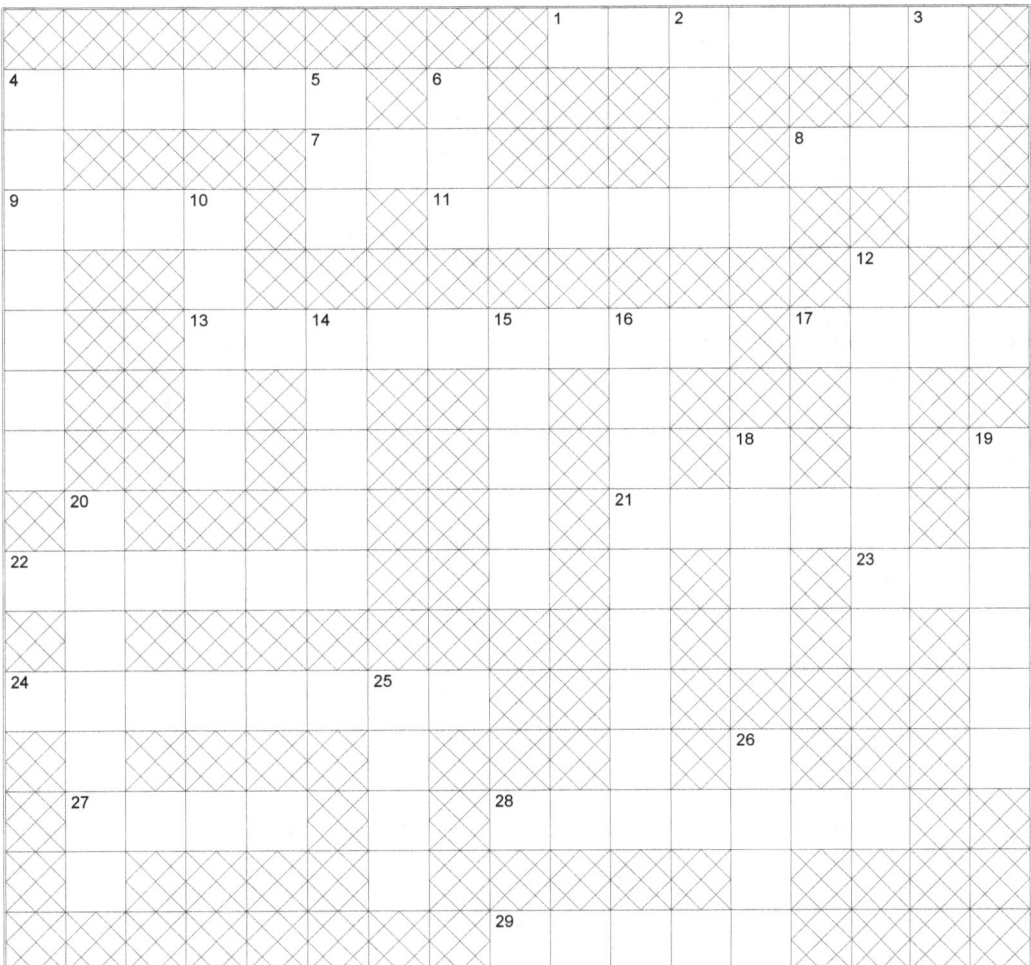

Across
1. Second kind of fish Santiago ate
4. Santiago's muscular problem with his hands
7. Santiago got a cut below his ____ when the fish pulled him over.
8. Baseball club
9. It holds a sail.
11. I know many ____ and I have resolution.
13. Santiago got his nickname from arm ____ in his youth.
17. Fish lure
21. The worst kind of bad luck
22. Loss
23. Santiago tied his knife to one to make a weapon.
24. The fish are our ____.
27. Santiago's home country
28. Leftover bones
29. Santiago's kind of boat

Down
2. Santiago had a streak of bad ____
3. Tied rope-like things that catch fish
4. The old man: El ____
5. Ocean
6. The fish's splash got Santiago all ____.
10. What the big fish did to Santiago's boat
12. Sharp instrument that finally killed the big fish
14. It is better to be lucky. But I would rather be ____
15. Subject of the old man's dreams
16. Daily news publication
18. Santiago hit the sharks with one.
19. Pub/restaurant owner
20. He received the head of the fish from Santiago
25. Yellow ____; a friendly, wishful joke
26. Large hook with which one pulls in a lined fish

The Old Man and The Sea Crossword 1 Answer Key

							¹D	O	L	P	H	I	³N	
⁴C	R	A	⁵M	P	⁶S				²U				E	
A			⁷E	Y	E				C		⁸B	A	T	
⁹M	A	¹⁰S	T		A		¹¹T	R	I	C	K	S		S
P		O									¹²H			
E		¹³W	¹⁴R	E	S	¹⁵T	L	¹⁶I	N	G	¹⁷B	A	I	T
O			E		X		I		E			R		
N			E		D		O		W		¹⁸C		P	¹⁹M
		²⁰P			C		N		²¹S	A	L	A	O	A
²²D	E	F	E	A	T		S		P		U		²³O	A	R
		D							A		B		N		T
²⁴B	R	O	T	H	²⁵E	R	S		P						I
		I			I				E		²⁶G				N
		²⁷C	U	B	A		²⁸C	A	R	C	A	S	S		
		O					E				F				
							²⁹S	K	I	F	F				

Across
1. Second kind of fish Santiago ate
4. Santiago's muscular problem with his hands
7. Santiago got a cut below his ____ when the fish pulled him over.
8. Baseball club
9. It holds a sail.
11. I know many ____ and I have resolution.
13. Santiago got his nickname from arm ____ in his youth.
17. Fish lure
21. The worst kind of bad luck
22. Loss
23. Santiago tied his knife to one to make a weapon.
24. The fish are our ____.
27. Santiago's home country
28. Leftover bones
29. Santiago's kind of boat

Down
2. Santiago had a streak of bad ____
3. Tied rope-like things that catch fish
4. The old man: El ____
5. Ocean
6. The fish's splash got Santiago all ____.
10. What the big fish did to Santiago's boat
12. Sharp instrument that finally killed the big fish
14. It is better to be lucky. But I would rather be ____
15. Subject of the old man's dreams
16. Daily news publication
18. Santiago hit the sharks with one.
19. Pub/restaurant owner
20. He received the head of the fish from Santiago
25. Yellow ____; a friendly, wishful joke
26. Large hook with which one pulls in a lined fish

The Old Man and The Sea Crossword 2

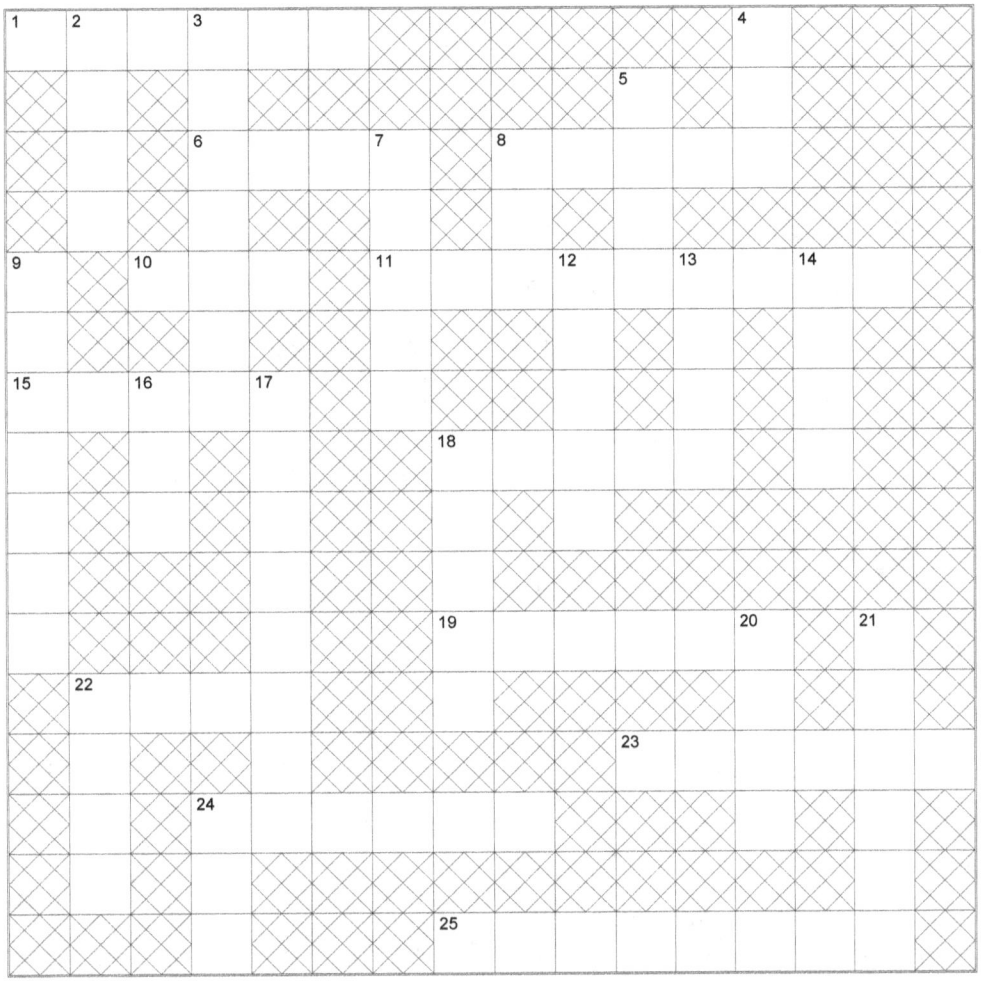

Across
1. I know many ____ and I have resolution.
6. It holds a sail.
8. It is better to be lucky. But I would rather be ____
10. Ocean
11. Santiago got his nickname from arm ____ in his youth.
15. Subject of the old man's dreams
18. Small house, usually run-down
19. Santiago ate ____ fish from the bigger fish's stomach.
22. Santiago's home country
23. Loss
24. Kind of tuna
25. The fish are our ____.

Down
2. Yellow ____; a friendly, wishful joke
3. The old man: El ___
4. The fish's splash got Santiago all ____.
5. Fish lure
7. What the big fish did to Santiago's boat
8. Santiago got a cut below his ____ when the fish pulled him over.
9. Second kind of fish Santiago ate
12. The worst kind of bad luck
13. Santiago had a streak of bad ____
14. Tied rope-like things that catch fish
16. Santiago tied his knife to one to make a weapon.
17. El Campeon; the old man
18. Santiago's kind of boat
20. Large hook with which one pulls in a lined fish
21. Santiago's muscular problem with his hands
22. Santiago hit the sharks with one.
24. Baseball club

The Old Man and The Sea Crossword 2 Answer Key

	1 T	2 R	3 I	C	K	S				4 W	
		I		A				5 B		E	
		C	6 M	A	S	7 T	8 E	X	A	C	T
		E		P		O		Y		I	
9 D		10 S	E	A		11 W	R	E	12 S	13 T	L	14 I	N	G
O				O			E		A		U		E	
15 L		16 I	O	17 N	S		D		L		C		T	
P		A		A			18 S	H	A	C	K		S	
H		R		N			K		O					
I				T			I							
N				I		19 F	L	Y	I	N	20 G		21 C	
		22 C	U	B	A		F				A		R	
		L		G					23 D	E	F	E	A	T
		U		24 B	O	N	I	T	O				M	
		B		A									P	
				T			25 B	R	O	T	H	E	R	S

Across
1. I know many ____ and I have resolution.
6. It holds a sail.
8. It is better to be lucky. But I would rather be ____
10. Ocean
11. Santiago got his nickname from arm ____ in his youth.
15. Subject of the old man's dreams
18. Small house, usually run-down
19. Santiago ate ____ fish from the bigger fish's stomach.
22. Santiago's home country
23. Loss
24. Kind of tuna
25. The fish are our ____.

Down
2. Yellow ____; a friendly, wishful joke
3. The old man: El ___
4. The fish's splash got Santiago all ____.
5. Fish lure
7. What the big fish did to Santiago's boat
8. Santiago got a cut below his ____ when the fish pulled him over.
9. Second kind of fish Santiago ate
12. The worst kind of bad luck
13. Santiago had a streak of bad ____
14. Tied rope-like things that catch fish
16. Santiago tied his knife to one to make a weapon.
17. El Campeon; the old man
18. Santiago's kind of boat
20. Large hook with which one pulls in a lined fish
21. Santiago's muscular problem with his hands
22. Santiago hit the sharks with one.
24. Baseball club

The Old Man and The Sea Crossword 3

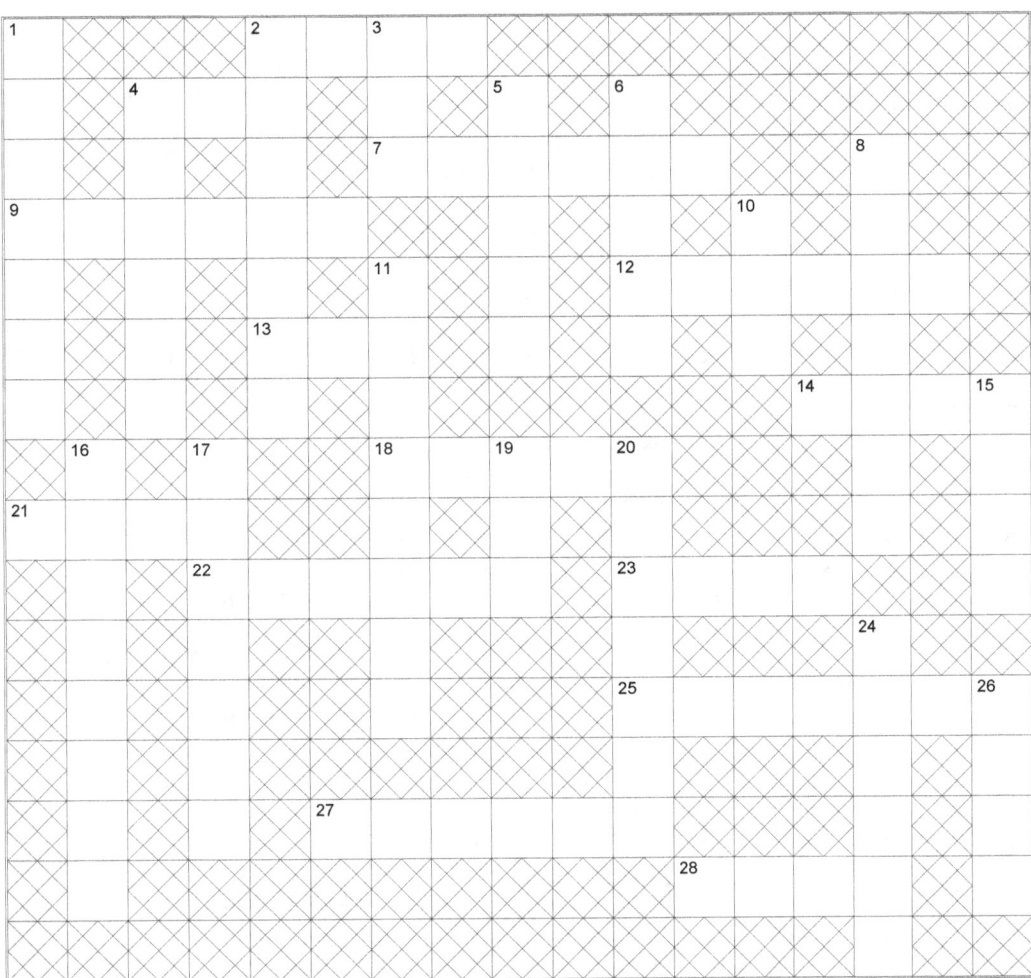

Across
2. Santiago's home country
4. Ocean
7. I know many ____ and I have resolution.
9. Santiago's muscular problem with his hands
12. Santiago ate ____ fish from the bigger fish's stomach.
13. Santiago tied his knife to one to make a weapon.
14. Santiago hit the sharks with one.
18. What the big fish did to Santiago's boat
21. Yellow ____; a friendly, wishful joke
22. Loss
23. Santiago had a streak of bad ____
25. Sharp instrument that finally killed the big fish
27. Pub/restaurant owner
28. It holds a sail.

Down
1. Leftover bones
2. The old man: El ___
3. Baseball club
4. They attacked and ate the big fish.
5. Subject of the old man's dreams
6. Santiago's kind of boat
8. The boy
10. Santiago got a cut below his ____ when the fish pulled him over.
11. The fish are our ____.
15. Fish lure
16. Baseball great
17. He received the head of the fish from Santiago
19. The fish's splash got Santiago all ____.
20. Second kind of fish Santiago ate
24. Kind of tuna
26. Tied rope-like things that catch fish

The Old Man and The Sea Crossword 3 Answer Key

	1 C		2 C	U	B	A						
	A		4 S	E	A		A		5 L		6 S	
	R		H		M		7 T	R	I	C	K	S		8 M
9 C	R	A	M	P	S				O		10 E		A
	A		R			11 B		N		12 F	L	Y	I	N	G
	S		K	13 O	A	R		S		F		E		O
	S		S		N		O					14 C	L	15 U	B
	16 D		17 P		18 T	O	W	19 E	20 D			I		A
21 R	I	C	E			H		E		O		N		I
	M		22 D	E	F	E	A	T		23 L	U	C	K		T
	A		R			R				P		24 B	
	G		I			S			25 H	A	R	P	O	O	26 N
	G		C						I			N		E
	I		O		27 M	A	R	T	I	N		I		T
	O								28 M	A	S	T		S
									O				

Across
2. Santiago's home country
4. Ocean
7. I know many ____ and I have resolution.
9. Santiago's muscular problem with his hands
12. Santiago ate ____ fish from the bigger fish's stomach.
13. Santiago tied his knife to one to make a weapon.
14. Santiago hit the sharks with one.
18. What the big fish did to Santiago's boat
21. Yellow ____; a friendly, wishful joke
22. Loss
23. Santiago had a streak of bad ____
25. Sharp instrument that finally killed the big fish
27. Pub/restaurant owner
28. It holds a sail.

Down
1. Leftover bones
2. The old man: El ___
3. Baseball club
4. They attacked and ate the big fish.
5. Subject of the old man's dreams
6. Santiago's kind of boat
8. The boy
10. Santiago got a cut below his ____ when the fish pulled him over.
11. The fish are our ____.
15. Fish lure
16. Baseball great
17. He received the head of the fish from Santiago
19. The fish's splash got Santiago all ____.
20. Second kind of fish Santiago ate
24. Kind of tuna
26. Tied rope-like things that catch fish

The Old Man and The Sea Crossword 4

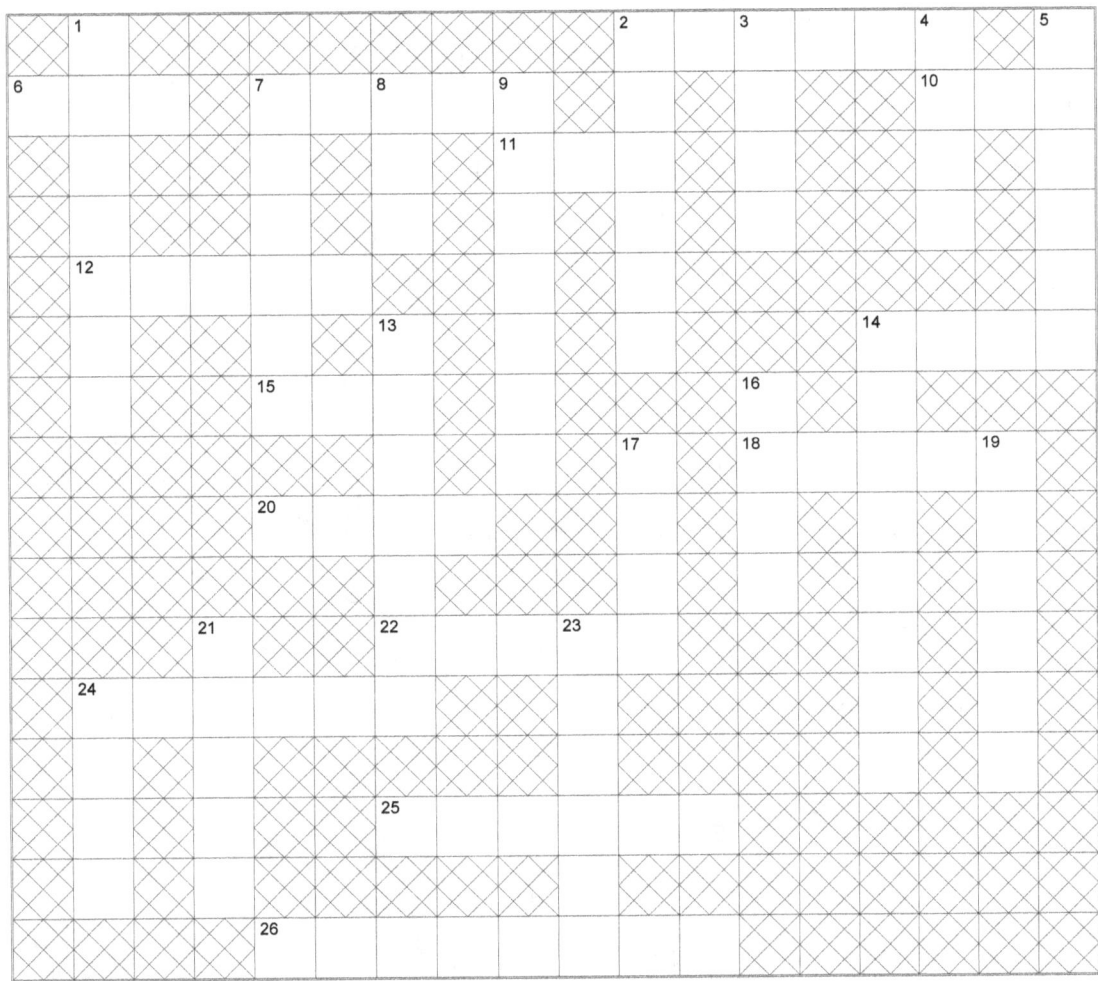

Across
2. Kind of fish the old man caught
6. Baseball club
7. What the big fish did to Santiago's boat
10. Santiago got a cut below his ____ when the fish pulled him over.
11. Santiago tied his knife to one to make a weapon.
12. It is better to be lucky. But I would rather be ____
14. Fish lure
15. Ocean
18. Subject of the old man's dreams
20. Santiago had a streak of bad ____
22. Santiago's kind of boat
24. Santiago's muscular problem with his hands
25. Kind of tuna
26. Baseball great

Down
1. The old man: El ___
2. Pub/restaurant owner
3. Yellow ____; a friendly, wishful joke
4. Tied rope-like things that catch fish
5. Loss
7. I know many ____ and I have resolution.
8. The fish's splash got Santiago all ____.
9. Second kind of fish Santiago ate
13. Leftover bones
14. The fish are our ____.
16. Santiago hit the sharks with one.
17. Large hook with which one pulls in a lined fish
19. They attacked and ate the big fish.
21. The worst kind of bad luck
23. Santiago ate ____ fish from the bigger fish's stomach.
24. Santiago's home country

The Old Man and The Sea Crossword 4 Answer Key

	1 C						2 M	3 A	R	L	4 I	N	5 D
6 B	A	T	7 T	8 O	9 W	E	D				10 E	Y	E
	M		R	E	11 O	A	R		C		T		F
	P		I	T	L		T		E		S		E
12 E	X	A	C	T		P		I					A
	O		K	13 C	H		N			14 B	A	I	T
	N		15 S	E	A			16 C		R			
				R	I	N	17 G	18 L	I	O	N	19 S	
			20 L	U	C	K		A	U	T		H	
				A				F	B		H	A	
		21 S		22 S	K	I	23 F	F			E	R	
	24 C	R	A	M	P	S		L			R	K	
	U	L						Y			S	S	
	B	A		25 B	O	N	I	T	O				
	A	O				N							
			26 D	I	M	A	G	G	I	O			

Across
2. Kind of fish the old man caught
6. Baseball club
7. What the big fish did to Santiago's boat
10. Santiago got a cut below his ____ when the fish pulled him over.
11. Santiago tied his knife to one to make a weapon.
12. It is better to be lucky. But I would rather be ____
14. Fish lure
15. Ocean
18. Subject of the old man's dreams
20. Santiago had a streak of bad ____
22. Santiago's kind of boat
24. Santiago's muscular problem with his hands
25. Kind of tuna
26. Baseball great

Down
1. The old man: El ___
2. Pub/restaurant owner
3. Yellow ____; a friendly, wishful joke
4. Tied rope-like things that catch fish
5. Loss
7. I know many ____ and I have resolution.
8. The fish's splash got Santiago all ____.
9. Second kind of fish Santiago ate
13. Leftover bones
14. The fish are our ____.
16. Santiago hit the sharks with one.
17. Large hook with which one pulls in a lined fish
19. They attacked and ate the big fish.
21. The worst kind of bad luck
23. Santiago ate ____ fish from the bigger fish's stomach.
24. Santiago's home country

The Old Man and The Sea

CRAMPS	BROTHERS	FLYING	LUCK	EXACT
MANOLIN	PEDRICO	BAIT	TRICKS	NETS
MARLIN	WET	FREE SPACE	SEA	CUBA
BAT	GAFF	DEFEAT	CLUB	TOWED
LIONS	OAR	NEWSPAPER	SKIFF	WRESTLING

The Old Man and The Sea

SALAO	DOLPHIN	BONITO	RICE	SANTIAGO
CARCASS	SHACK	CAMPEON	HARPOON	SHARKS
DIMAGGIO	MAST	FREE SPACE	WRESTLING	SKIFF
NEWSPAPER	OAR	LIONS	TOWED	CLUB
DEFEAT	GAFF	BAT	CUBA	SEA

The Old Man and The Sea

NEWSPAPER	LUCK	BONITO	DEFEAT	FLYING
CRAMPS	TRICKS	BAT	NETS	BAIT
MANOLIN	TOWED	FREE SPACE	CUBA	MARTIN
DOLPHIN	PEDRICO	MARLIN	EYE	OAR
LIONS	DIMAGGIO	WRESTLING	SALAO	CLUB

The Old Man and The Sea

SKIFF	GAFF	SANTIAGO	SHARKS	SEA
RICE	MAST	WET	BROTHERS	CAMPEON
EXACT	SHACK	FREE SPACE	CLUB	SALAO
WRESTLING	DIMAGGIO	LIONS	OAR	EYE
MARLIN	PEDRICO	DOLPHIN	MARTIN	CUBA

The Old Man and The Sea

MANOLIN	LUCK	LIONS	DIMAGGIO	SANTIAGO
NEWSPAPER	NETS	MAST	DEFEAT	SALAO
BAIT	SHARKS	FREE SPACE	EXACT	WET
BROTHERS	TOWED	CARCASS	CRAMPS	RICE
TRICKS	BONITO	OAR	PEDRICO	EYE

The Old Man and The Sea

SKIFF	SEA	CAMPEON	MARLIN	SHACK
CUBA	DOLPHIN	HARPOON	GAFF	BAT
WRESTLING	FLYING	FREE SPACE	EYE	PEDRICO
OAR	BONITO	TRICKS	RICE	CRAMPS
CARCASS	TOWED	BROTHERS	WET	EXACT

The Old Man and The Sea

NETS	OAR	FLYING	EYE	CARCASS
DOLPHIN	BONITO	RICE	SANTIAGO	BROTHERS
SHARKS	CUBA	FREE SPACE	GAFF	CLUB
EXACT	BAT	MANOLIN	CRAMPS	PEDRICO
MAST	MARLIN	MARTIN	SALAO	LUCK

The Old Man and The Sea

TRICKS	NEWSPAPER	SKIFF	WET	CAMPEON
HARPOON	DEFEAT	LIONS	TOWED	DIMAGGIO
SHACK	BAIT	FREE SPACE	LUCK	SALAO
MARTIN	MARLIN	MAST	PEDRICO	CRAMPS
MANOLIN	BAT	EXACT	CLUB	GAFF

The Old Man and The Sea

GAFF	CLUB	SANTIAGO	SHACK	EYE
EXACT	OAR	CUBA	HARPOON	WET
SEA	PEDRICO	FREE SPACE	LUCK	DIMAGGIO
MANOLIN	DEFEAT	MARTIN	CARCASS	WRESTLING
DOLPHIN	TOWED	MAST	TRICKS	CRAMPS

The Old Man and The Sea

SHARKS	MARLIN	BONITO	NETS	NEWSPAPER
LIONS	SALAO	CAMPEON	RICE	SKIFF
BAT	BROTHERS	FREE SPACE	CRAMPS	TRICKS
MAST	TOWED	DOLPHIN	WRESTLING	CARCASS
MARTIN	DEFEAT	MANOLIN	DIMAGGIO	LUCK

The Old Man and The Sea

TRICKS	WRESTLING	BAIT	CARCASS	CLUB
MAST	NEWSPAPER	HARPOON	RICE	BONITO
BROTHERS	MANOLIN	FREE SPACE	LUCK	EXACT
EYE	MARLIN	PEDRICO	DIMAGGIO	BAT
WET	FLYING	SHARKS	SANTIAGO	GAFF

The Old Man and The Sea

NETS	CAMPEON	SHACK	CRAMPS	SALAO
DOLPHIN	SEA	SKIFF	DEFEAT	CUBA
MARTIN	OAR	FREE SPACE	GAFF	SANTIAGO
SHARKS	FLYING	WET	BAT	DIMAGGIO
PEDRICO	MARLIN	EYE	EXACT	LUCK

The Old Man and The Sea

SEA	BONITO	BAIT	CUBA	CARCASS
TRICKS	SHACK	GAFF	HARPOON	TOWED
SHARKS	WET	FREE SPACE	FLYING	DIMAGGIO
CLUB	NETS	CAMPEON	PEDRICO	DOLPHIN
SANTIAGO	SKIFF	MANOLIN	MAST	CRAMPS

The Old Man and The Sea

LUCK	LIONS	DEFEAT	BAT	OAR
MARLIN	EYE	WRESTLING	RICE	BROTHERS
EXACT	MARTIN	FREE SPACE	CRAMPS	MAST
MANOLIN	SKIFF	SANTIAGO	DOLPHIN	PEDRICO
CAMPEON	NETS	CLUB	DIMAGGIO	FLYING

The Old Man and The Sea

FLYING	TOWED	RICE	OAR	SALAO
LUCK	HARPOON	MARTIN	BONITO	BROTHERS
TRICKS	EYE	FREE SPACE	BAT	MAST
CRAMPS	MANOLIN	WET	SANTIAGO	SKIFF
LIONS	PEDRICO	BAIT	SEA	NETS

The Old Man and The Sea

CLUB	DOLPHIN	GAFF	CUBA	SHACK
MARLIN	DIMAGGIO	NEWSPAPER	EXACT	DEFEAT
WRESTLING	CARCASS	FREE SPACE	NETS	SEA
BAIT	PEDRICO	LIONS	SKIFF	SANTIAGO
WET	MANOLIN	CRAMPS	MAST	BAT

The Old Man and The Sea

SANTIAGO	EXACT	MANOLIN	OAR	CRAMPS
MAST	BROTHERS	BONITO	NEWSPAPER	EYE
WRESTLING	DOLPHIN	FREE SPACE	PEDRICO	RICE
NETS	GAFF	TRICKS	BAT	LUCK
SKIFF	TOWED	CAMPEON	FLYING	SEA

The Old Man and The Sea

WET	CARCASS	CUBA	LIONS	MARLIN
DEFEAT	BAIT	SALAO	DIMAGGIO	SHACK
MARTIN	SHARKS	FREE SPACE	SEA	FLYING
CAMPEON	TOWED	SKIFF	LUCK	BAT
TRICKS	GAFF	NETS	RICE	PEDRICO

The Old Man and The Sea

SKIFF	SALAO	WRESTLING	BAT	MAST
CUBA	OAR	LUCK	DIMAGGIO	CRAMPS
LIONS	SANTIAGO	FREE SPACE	BROTHERS	RICE
TRICKS	WET	SHARKS	EXACT	HARPOON
BAIT	MANOLIN	FLYING	EYE	CARCASS

The Old Man and The Sea

SHACK	BONITO	PEDRICO	NEWSPAPER	DOLPHIN
SEA	NETS	MARLIN	TOWED	GAFF
CAMPEON	DEFEAT	FREE SPACE	CARCASS	EYE
FLYING	MANOLIN	BAIT	HARPOON	EXACT
SHARKS	WET	TRICKS	RICE	BROTHERS

The Old Man and The Sea

CRAMPS	BROTHERS	PEDRICO	EYE	TRICKS
MARLIN	BONITO	SKIFF	MAST	EXACT
SHACK	BAT	FREE SPACE	DIMAGGIO	LUCK
CLUB	FLYING	SHARKS	SANTIAGO	NEWSPAPER
LIONS	MARTIN	CARCASS	RICE	WET

The Old Man and The Sea

DOLPHIN	SEA	MANOLIN	WRESTLING	CUBA
OAR	GAFF	BAIT	DEFEAT	CAMPEON
HARPOON	SALAO	FREE SPACE	WET	RICE
CARCASS	MARTIN	LIONS	NEWSPAPER	SANTIAGO
SHARKS	FLYING	CLUB	LUCK	DIMAGGIO

Copyrighted

The Old Man and The Sea

OAR	CRAMPS	DEFEAT	SANTIAGO	HARPOON
SKIFF	SHARKS	CLUB	SHACK	DOLPHIN
NETS	CARCASS	FREE SPACE	SALAO	MAST
MANOLIN	BONITO	FLYING	BAT	EXACT
GAFF	BROTHERS	RICE	LUCK	PEDRICO

The Old Man and The Sea

CAMPEON	EYE	WRESTLING	CUBA	TOWED
MARLIN	WET	LIONS	SEA	MARTIN
BAIT	DIMAGGIO	FREE SPACE	PEDRICO	LUCK
RICE	BROTHERS	GAFF	EXACT	BAT
FLYING	BONITO	MANOLIN	MAST	SALAO

The Old Man and The Sea

FLYING	SALAO	DEFEAT	CARCASS	BAT
PEDRICO	EXACT	WET	LUCK	MAST
CUBA	DOLPHIN	FREE SPACE	RICE	TRICKS
SHARKS	MANOLIN	HARPOON	NEWSPAPER	CLUB
WRESTLING	SEA	LIONS	NETS	SHACK

The Old Man and The Sea

BROTHERS	OAR	GAFF	CRAMPS	MARLIN
DIMAGGIO	CAMPEON	SANTIAGO	BAIT	SKIFF
TOWED	BONITO	FREE SPACE	SHACK	NETS
LIONS	SEA	WRESTLING	CLUB	NEWSPAPER
HARPOON	MANOLIN	SHARKS	TRICKS	RICE

The Old Man and The Sea

CRAMPS	LUCK	SANTIAGO	DOLPHIN	MARLIN
CAMPEON	BROTHERS	OAR	DIMAGGIO	WET
LIONS	SHARKS	FREE SPACE	SALAO	WRESTLING
MAST	MANOLIN	TRICKS	GAFF	SHACK
PEDRICO	FLYING	CARCASS	SKIFF	EXACT

The Old Man and The Sea

BAIT	BAT	NEWSPAPER	TOWED	DEFEAT
CLUB	RICE	HARPOON	CUBA	NETS
EYE	SEA	FREE SPACE	EXACT	SKIFF
CARCASS	FLYING	PEDRICO	SHACK	GAFF
TRICKS	MANOLIN	MAST	WRESTLING	SALAO

The Old Man and The Sea

CARCASS	MARLIN	CRAMPS	CUBA	BONITO
NETS	SHACK	MAST	DIMAGGIO	SKIFF
TRICKS	WET	FREE SPACE	RICE	SEA
BAT	MANOLIN	HARPOON	PEDRICO	SANTIAGO
CAMPEON	EXACT	NEWSPAPER	TOWED	SHARKS

The Old Man and The Sea

BAIT	WRESTLING	SALAO	GAFF	DOLPHIN
LUCK	DEFEAT	BROTHERS	FLYING	OAR
CLUB	EYE	FREE SPACE	SHARKS	TOWED
NEWSPAPER	EXACT	CAMPEON	SANTIAGO	PEDRICO
HARPOON	MANOLIN	BAT	SEA	RICE

The Old Man and The Sea

NETS	SHACK	GAFF	OAR	SANTIAGO
WET	FLYING	PEDRICO	TOWED	BROTHERS
SALAO	CAMPEON	FREE SPACE	SHARKS	BAT
DIMAGGIO	CUBA	HARPOON	SKIFF	CARCASS
BONITO	EYE	CLUB	MANOLIN	LIONS

The Old Man and The Sea

DOLPHIN	WRESTLING	RICE	DEFEAT	TRICKS
BAIT	SEA	MARLIN	LUCK	NEWSPAPER
CRAMPS	MARTIN	FREE SPACE	LIONS	MANOLIN
CLUB	EYE	BONITO	CARCASS	SKIFF
HARPOON	CUBA	DIMAGGIO	BAT	SHARKS

Old Man & The Sea Vocabulary Word List

No.	Word	Clue/Definition
1.	ATTAINED	Gained as an objective; achieved
2.	BENEVOLENT	Characterized by or suggestive of doing good
3.	COMMENCED	Began; started
4.	CONGREGATED	Gathered; assembled
5.	CONTEMPT	Scorn; disparaging or haughty disdain
6.	CONVULSIVELY	Shaking or agitating violently with irregular and involuntary muscular contractions
7.	DEVISE	To form, plan, or arrange in one's mind; design or contrive
8.	ENDURES	To carry on through despite hardships
9.	FATHOMS	Units of length equal to six feet
10.	FURLED	Rolled up and secured to something
11.	HUMILIATING	Lowering the pride, dignity or self-respect
12.	HUMILITY	Marked by meekness or modesty in behavior
13.	IMMUNE	Not affected by a given influence; unresponsive
14.	INEFFECTUAL	Insufficient to produce a desired effect
15.	INTOLERABLE	Unbearable
16.	IRIDESCENT	Producing a display of lustrous, rainbowlike colors
17.	MALIGNANCY	Something disposed to do evil; highly injurious
18.	MUTILATED	Disfigured beyond repair
19.	PHOSPHORESCENCE	Emission of light without burning
20.	PLACID	Calm; quiet
21.	PROLONGS	To lengthen in duration; protract
22.	RAPIER	A light, sharp-pointed sword lacking a cutting edge and used only for thrusting
23.	RESOLUTION	Firm determination
24.	SCAVENGER	An animal that feeds on decaying matter
25.	SUSTENANCE	Something, esp. food, that sustains life or health
26.	THWART	A seat across a boat on which a rower may sit
27.	VIOLATED	Broke or disregarded

Old Man & The Sea Vocabulary Fill In The Blanks 1

_____ 1. Insufficient to produce a desired effect

_____ 2. Began; started

_____ 3. Gathered; assembled

_____ 4. Marked by meekness or modesty in behavior

_____ 5. Shaking or agitating violently with irregular and involuntary muscular contractions

_____ 6. Producing a display of lustrous, rainbowlike colors

_____ 7. Characterized by or suggestive of doing good

_____ 8. To form, plan, or arrange in one's mind; design or contrive

_____ 9. Rolled up and secured to something

_____ 10. Not affected by a given influence; unresponsive

_____ 11. Broke or disregarded

_____ 12. Scorn; disparaging or haughty disdain

_____ 13. Firm determination

_____ 14. A seat across a boat on which a rower may sit

_____ 15. To lengthen in duration; protract

_____ 16. Something, esp. food, that sustains life or health

_____ 17. Lowering the pride, dignity or self-respect

_____ 18. Gained as an objective; achieved

_____ 19. Unbearable

_____ 20. Something disposed to do evil; highly injurious

Old Man & The Sea Vocabulary Fill In The Blanks 1 Answer Key

INEFFECTUAL	1. Insufficient to produce a desired effect
COMMENCED	2. Began; started
CONGREGATED	3. Gathered; assembled
HUMILITY	4. Marked by meekness or modesty in behavior
CONVULSIVELY	5. Shaking or agitating violently with irregular and involuntary muscular contractions
IRIDESCENT	6. Producing a display of lustrous, rainbowlike colors
BENEVOLENT	7. Characterized by or suggestive of doing good
DEVISE	8. To form, plan, or arrange in one's mind; design or contrive
FURLED	9. Rolled up and secured to something
IMMUNE	10. Not affected by a given influence; unresponsive
VIOLATED	11. Broke or disregarded
CONTEMPT	12. Scorn; disparaging or haughty disdain
RESOLUTION	13. Firm determination
THWART	14. A seat across a boat on which a rower may sit
PROLONGS	15. To lengthen in duration; protract
SUSTENANCE	16. Something, esp. food, that sustains life or health
HUMILIATING	17. Lowering the pride, dignity or self-respect
ATTAINED	18. Gained as an objective; achieved
INTOLERABLE	19. Unbearable
MALIGNANCY	20. Something disposed to do evil; highly injurious

Old Man & The Sea Vocabulary Fill In The Blanks 2

1. A light, sharp-pointed sword lacking a cutting edge and used only for thrusting
2. Something disposed to do evil; highly injurious
3. To lengthen in duration; protract
4. Scorn; disparaging or haughty disdain
5. Characterized by or suggestive of doing good
6. Broke or disregarded
7. An animal that feeds on decaying matter
8. Emission of light without burning
9. Gained as an objective; achieved
10. To form, plan, or arrange in one's mind; design or contrive
11. Began; started
12. Producing a display of lustrous, rainbowlike colors
13. Marked by meekness or modesty in behavior
14. Insufficient to produce a desired effect
15. Not affected by a given influence; unresponsive
16. Shaking or agitating violently with irregular and involuntary muscular contractions
17. Calm; quiet
18. Unbearable
19. Gathered; assembled
20. A seat across a boat on which a rower may sit

Old Man & The Sea Vocabulary Fill In The Blanks 2 Answer Key

RAPIER	1. A light, sharp-pointed sword lacking a cutting edge and used only for thrusting
MALIGNANCY	2. Something disposed to do evil; highly injurious
PROLONGS	3. To lengthen in duration; protract
CONTEMPT	4. Scorn; disparaging or haughty disdain
BENEVOLENT	5. Characterized by or suggestive of doing good
VIOLATED	6. Broke or disregarded
SCAVENGER	7. An animal that feeds on decaying matter
PHOSPHORESCENCE	8. Emission of light without burning
ATTAINED	9. Gained as an objective; achieved
DEVISE	10. To form, plan, or arrange in one's mind; design or contrive
COMMENCED	11. Began; started
IRIDESCENT	12. Producing a display of lustrous, rainbowlike colors
HUMILITY	13. Marked by meekness or modesty in behavior
INEFFECTUAL	14. Insufficient to produce a desired effect
IMMUNE	15. Not affected by a given influence; unresponsive
CONVULSIVELY	16. Shaking or agitating violently with irregular and involuntary muscular contractions
PLACID	17. Calm; quiet
INTOLERABLE	18. Unbearable
CONGREGATED	19. Gathered; assembled
THWART	20. A seat across a boat on which a rower may sit

Old Man & The Sea Vocabulary Fill In The Blanks 3

1. To form, plan, or arrange in one's mind; design or contrive
2. Marked by meekness or modesty in behavior
3. Something disposed to do evil; highly injurious
4. A light, sharp-pointed sword lacking a cutting edge and used only for thrusting
5. To lengthen in duration; protract
6. Firm determination
7. Unbearable
8. Insufficient to produce a desired effect
9. Scorn; disparaging or haughty disdain
10. Not affected by a given influence; unresponsive
11. Shaking or agitating violently with irregular and involuntary muscular contractions
12. Lowering the pride, dignity or self-respect
13. Something, esp. food, that sustains life or health
14. Rolled up and secured to something
15. Disfigured beyond repair
16. Calm; quiet
17. Units of length equal to six feet
18. Gathered; assembled
19. Emission of light without burning
20. An animal that feeds on decaying matter

Old Man & The Sea Vocabulary Fill In The Blanks 3 Answer Key

DEVISE	1. To form, plan, or arrange in one's mind; design or contrive
HUMILITY	2. Marked by meekness or modesty in behavior
MALIGNANCY	3. Something disposed to do evil; highly injurious
RAPIER	4. A light, sharp-pointed sword lacking a cutting edge and used only for thrusting
PROLONGS	5. To lengthen in duration; protract
RESOLUTION	6. Firm determination
INTOLERABLE	7. Unbearable
INEFFECTUAL	8. Insufficient to produce a desired effect
CONTEMPT	9. Scorn; disparaging or haughty disdain
IMMUNE	10. Not affected by a given influence; unresponsive
CONVULSIVELY	11. Shaking or agitating violently with irregular and involuntary muscular contractions
HUMILIATING	12. Lowering the pride, dignity or self-respect
SUSTENANCE	13. Something, esp. food, that sustains life or health
FURLED	14. Rolled up and secured to something
MUTILATED	15. Disfigured beyond repair
PLACID	16. Calm; quiet
FATHOMS	17. Units of length equal to six feet
CONGREGATED	18. Gathered; assembled
PHOSPHORESCENCE	19. Emission of light without burning
SCAVENGER	20. An animal that feeds on decaying matter

Old Man & The Sea Vocabulary Fill In The Blanks 4

_____ 1. Gained as an objective; achieved

_____ 2. Emission of light without burning

_____ 3. Broke or disregarded

_____ 4. Began; started

_____ 5. Something disposed to do evil; highly injurious

_____ 6. To form, plan, or arrange in one's mind; design or contrive

_____ 7. Insufficient to produce a desired effect

_____ 8. To lengthen in duration; protract

_____ 9. Characterized by or suggestive of doing good

_____ 10. To carry on through despite hardships

_____ 11. Not affected by a given influence; unresponsive

_____ 12. A seat across a boat on which a rower may sit

_____ 13. Scorn; disparaging or haughty disdain

_____ 14. Lowering the pride, dignity or self-respect

_____ 15. A light, sharp-pointed sword lacking a cutting edge and used only for thrusting

_____ 16. Calm; quiet

_____ 17. Unbearable

_____ 18. Producing a display of lustrous, rainbowlike colors

_____ 19. Something, esp. food, that sustains life or health

_____ 20. Firm determination

Old Man & The Sea Vocabulary Fill In The Blanks 4 Answer Key

ATTAINED	1.	Gained as an objective; achieved
PHOSPHORESCENCE	2.	Emission of light without burning
VIOLATED	3.	Broke or disregarded
COMMENCED	4.	Began; started
MALIGNANCY	5.	Something disposed to do evil; highly injurious
DEVISE	6.	To form, plan, or arrange in one's mind; design or contrive
INEFFECTUAL	7.	Insufficient to produce a desired effect
PROLONGS	8.	To lengthen in duration; protract
BENEVOLENT	9.	Characterized by or suggestive of doing good
ENDURES	10.	To carry on through despite hardships
IMMUNE	11.	Not affected by a given influence; unresponsive
THWART	12.	A seat across a boat on which a rower may sit
CONTEMPT	13.	Scorn; disparaging or haughty disdain
HUMILIATING	14.	Lowering the pride, dignity or self-respect
RAPIER	15.	A light, sharp-pointed sword lacking a cutting edge and used only for thrusting
PLACID	16.	Calm; quiet
INTOLERABLE	17.	Unbearable
IRIDESCENT	18.	Producing a display of lustrous, rainbowlike colors
SUSTENANCE	19.	Something, esp. food, that sustains life or health
RESOLUTION	20.	Firm determination

Copyrighted

Old Man & The Sea Vocabulary Matching 1

___ 1. FATHOMS
___ 2. ENDURES
___ 3. PHOSPHORESCENCE
___ 4. INTOLERABLE
___ 5. SUSTENANCE
___ 6. SCAVENGER
___ 7. THWART
___ 8. RAPIER
___ 9. PLACID
___ 10. HUMILIATING
___ 11. CONGREGATED
___ 12. MALIGNANCY
___ 13. BENEVOLENT
___ 14. COMMENCED
___ 15. VIOLATED
___ 16. CONTEMPT
___ 17. PROLONGS
___ 18. RESOLUTION
___ 19. FURLED
___ 20. IRIDESCENT
___ 21. MUTILATED
___ 22. INEFFECTUAL
___ 23. CONVULSIVELY
___ 24. ATTAINED
___ 25. DEVISE

A. Emission of light without burning
B. Something, esp. food, that sustains life or health
C. Producing a display of lustrous, rainbowlike colors
D. Characterized by or suggestive of doing good
E. Units of length equal to six feet
F. Firm determination
G. To lengthen in duration; protract
H. Something disposed to do evil; highly injurious
I. Lowering the pride, dignity or self-respect
J. A light, sharp-pointed sword lacking a cutting edge and used only for thrusting
K. Disfigured beyond repair
L. Began; started
M. To form, plan, or arrange in one's mind; design or contrive
N. Gathered; assembled
O. Rolled up and secured to something
P. Insufficient to produce a desired effect
Q. Unbearable
R. Broke or disregarded
S. Scorn; disparaging or haughty disdain
T. A seat across a boat on which a rower may sit
U. Shaking or agitating violently with irregular and involuntary muscular contractions
V. An animal that feeds on decaying matter
W. Calm; quiet
X. Gained as an objective; achieved
Y. To carry on through despite hardships

Old Man & The Sea Vocabulary Matching 1 Answer Key

E - 1. FATHOMS
Y - 2. ENDURES
A - 3. PHOSPHORESCENCE
Q - 4. INTOLERABLE
B - 5. SUSTENANCE
V - 6. SCAVENGER
T - 7. THWART
J - 8. RAPIER
W - 9. PLACID
I - 10. HUMILIATING
N - 11. CONGREGATED
H - 12. MALIGNANCY
D - 13. BENEVOLENT
L - 14. COMMENCED
R - 15. VIOLATED
S - 16. CONTEMPT
G - 17. PROLONGS
F - 18. RESOLUTION
O - 19. FURLED
C - 20. IRIDESCENT
K - 21. MUTILATED
P - 22. INEFFECTUAL
U - 23. CONVULSIVELY
X - 24. ATTAINED
M - 25. DEVISE

A. Emission of light without burning
B. Something, esp. food, that sustains life or health
C. Producing a display of lustrous, rainbowlike colors
D. Characterized by or suggestive of doing good
E. Units of length equal to six feet
F. Firm determination
G. To lengthen in duration; protract
H. Something disposed to do evil; highly injurious
I. Lowering the pride, dignity or self-respect
J. A light, sharp-pointed sword lacking a cutting edge and used only for thrusting
K. Disfigured beyond repair
L. Began; started
M. To form, plan, or arrange in one's mind; design or contrive
N. Gathered; assembled
O. Rolled up and secured to something
P. Insufficient to produce a desired effect
Q. Unbearable
R. Broke or disregarded
S. Scorn; disparaging or haughty disdain
T. A seat across a boat on which a rower may sit
U. Shaking or agitating violently with irregular and involuntary muscular contractions
V. An animal that feeds on decaying matter
W. Calm; quiet
X. Gained as an objective; achieved
Y. To carry on through despite hardships

Old Man & The Sea Vocabulary Matching 2

___ 1. THWART
___ 2. CONTEMPT
___ 3. HUMILIATING
___ 4. INEFFECTUAL
___ 5. FURLED
___ 6. PLACID
___ 7. CONVULSIVELY
___ 8. RAPIER
___ 9. MALIGNANCY
___ 10. IMMUNE
___ 11. MUTILATED
___ 12. INTOLERABLE
___ 13. CONGREGATED
___ 14. SUSTENANCE
___ 15. VIOLATED
___ 16. DEVISE
___ 17. PHOSPHORESCENCE
___ 18. ENDURES
___ 19. SCAVENGER
___ 20. FATHOMS
___ 21. HUMILITY
___ 22. BENEVOLENT
___ 23. RESOLUTION
___ 24. PROLONGS
___ 25. ATTAINED

A. To lengthen in duration; protract
B. Lowering the pride, dignity or self-respect
C. Shaking or agitating violently with irregular and involuntary muscular contractions
D. Gained as an objective; achieved
E. Disfigured beyond repair
F. Insufficient to produce a desired effect
G. An animal that feeds on decaying matter
H. Scorn; disparaging or haughty disdain
I. Calm; quiet
J. To form, plan, or arrange in one's mind; design or contrive
K. Unbearable
L. Not affected by a given influence; unresponsive
M. Broke or disregarded
N. Emission of light without burning
O. A light, sharp-pointed sword lacking a cutting edge and used only for thrusting
P. To carry on through despite hardships
Q. Something disposed to do evil; highly injurious
R. Characterized by or suggestive of doing good
S. Firm determination
T. Units of length equal to six feet
U. Rolled up and secured to something
V. Marked by meekness or modesty in behavior
W. A seat across a boat on which a rower may sit
X. Gathered; assembled
Y. Something, esp. food, that sustains life or health

Old Man & The Sea Vocabulary Matching 2 Answer Key

W - 1.	THWART	A.	To lengthen in duration; protract
H - 2.	CONTEMPT	B.	Lowering the pride, dignity or self-respect
B - 3.	HUMILIATING	C.	Shaking or agitating violently with irregular and involuntary muscular contractions
F - 4.	INEFFECTUAL	D.	Gained as an objective; achieved
U - 5.	FURLED	E.	Disfigured beyond repair
I - 6.	PLACID	F.	Insufficient to produce a desired effect
C - 7.	CONVULSIVELY	G.	An animal that feeds on decaying matter
O - 8.	RAPIER	H.	Scorn; disparaging or haughty disdain
Q - 9.	MALIGNANCY	I.	Calm; quiet
L - 10.	IMMUNE	J.	To form, plan, or arrange in one's mind; design or contrive
E - 11.	MUTILATED	K.	Unbearable
K - 12.	INTOLERABLE	L.	Not affected by a given influence; unresponsive
X - 13.	CONGREGATED	M.	Broke or disregarded
Y - 14.	SUSTENANCE	N.	Emission of light without burning
M - 15.	VIOLATED	O.	A light, sharp-pointed sword lacking a cutting edge and used only for thrusting
J - 16.	DEVISE	P.	To carry on through despite hardships
N - 17.	PHOSPHORESCENCE	Q.	Something disposed to do evil; highly injurious
P - 18.	ENDURES	R.	Characterized by or suggestive of doing good
G - 19.	SCAVENGER	S.	Firm determination
T - 20.	FATHOMS	T.	Units of length equal to six feet
V - 21.	HUMILITY	U.	Rolled up and secured to something
R - 22.	BENEVOLENT	V.	Marked by meekness or modesty in behavior
S - 23.	RESOLUTION	W.	A seat across a boat on which a rower may sit
A - 24.	PROLONGS	X.	Gathered; assembled
D - 25.	ATTAINED	Y.	Something, esp. food, that sustains life or health

Old Man & The Sea Vocabulary Matching 3

___ 1. FURLED
___ 2. HUMILIATING
___ 3. RESOLUTION
___ 4. CONVULSIVELY
___ 5. PLACID
___ 6. DEVISE
___ 7. SUSTENANCE
___ 8. VIOLATED
___ 9. BENEVOLENT
___10. ATTAINED
___11. ENDURES
___12. MALIGNANCY
___13. CONGREGATED
___14. PHOSPHORESCENCE
___15. RAPIER
___16. SCAVENGER
___17. IMMUNE
___18. COMMENCED
___19. IRIDESCENT
___20. PROLONGS
___21. FATHOMS
___22. CONTEMPT
___23. THWART
___24. MUTILATED
___25. INEFFECTUAL

A. To form, plan, or arrange in one's mind; design or contrive
B. Gathered; assembled
C. Broke or disregarded
D. Rolled up and secured to something
E. A seat across a boat on which a rower may sit
F. Emission of light without burning
G. Began; started
H. Something, esp. food, that sustains life or health
I. A light, sharp-pointed sword lacking a cutting edge and used only for thrusting
J. Lowering the pride, dignity or self-respect
K. Disfigured beyond repair
L. Characterized by or suggestive of doing good
M. Shaking or agitating violently with irregular and involuntary muscular contractions
N. To carry on through despite hardships
O. Producing a display of lustrous, rainbowlike colors
P. Scorn; disparaging or haughty disdain
Q. Gained as an objective; achieved
R. Not affected by a given influence; unresponsive
S. Units of length equal to six feet
T. To lengthen in duration; protract
U. Firm determination
V. Something disposed to do evil; highly injurious
W. Calm; quiet
X. Insufficient to produce a desired effect
Y. An animal that feeds on decaying matter

Old Man & The Sea Vocabulary Matching 3 Answer Key

D - 1. FURLED	A.	To form, plan, or arrange in one's mind; design or contrive
J - 2. HUMILIATING	B.	Gathered; assembled
U - 3. RESOLUTION	C.	Broke or disregarded
M - 4. CONVULSIVELY	D.	Rolled up and secured to something
W - 5. PLACID	E.	A seat across a boat on which a rower may sit
A - 6. DEVISE	F.	Emission of light without burning
H - 7. SUSTENANCE	G.	Began; started
C - 8. VIOLATED	H.	Something, esp. food, that sustains life or health
L - 9. BENEVOLENT	I.	A light, sharp-pointed sword lacking a cutting edge and used only for thrusting
Q - 10. ATTAINED	J.	Lowering the pride, dignity or self-respect
N - 11. ENDURES	K.	Disfigured beyond repair
V - 12. MALIGNANCY	L.	Characterized by or suggestive of doing good
B - 13. CONGREGATED	M.	Shaking or agitating violently with irregular and involuntary muscular contractions
F - 14. PHOSPHORESCENCE	N.	To carry on through despite hardships
I - 15. RAPIER	O.	Producing a display of lustrous, rainbowlike colors
Y - 16. SCAVENGER	P.	Scorn; disparaging or haughty disdain
R - 17. IMMUNE	Q.	Gained as an objective; achieved
G - 18. COMMENCED	R.	Not affected by a given influence; unresponsive
O - 19. IRIDESCENT	S.	Units of length equal to six feet
T - 20. PROLONGS	T.	To lengthen in duration; protract
S - 21. FATHOMS	U.	Firm determination
P - 22. CONTEMPT	V.	Something disposed to do evil; highly injurious
E - 23. THWART	W.	Calm; quiet
K - 24. MUTILATED	X.	Insufficient to produce a desired effect
X - 25. INEFFECTUAL	Y.	An animal that feeds on decaying matter

Old Man & The Sea Vocabulary Matching 4

___ 1. DEVISE
___ 2. IMMUNE
___ 3. ATTAINED
___ 4. ENDURES
___ 5. FURLED
___ 6. IRIDESCENT
___ 7. RAPIER
___ 8. RESOLUTION
___ 9. CONTEMPT
___ 10. COMMENCED
___ 11. PLACID
___ 12. MUTILATED
___ 13. SUSTENANCE
___ 14. HUMILITY
___ 15. BENEVOLENT
___ 16. THWART
___ 17. CONVULSIVELY
___ 18. PHOSPHORESCENCE
___ 19. INTOLERABLE
___ 20. HUMILIATING
___ 21. SCAVENGER
___ 22. MALIGNANCY
___ 23. CONGREGATED
___ 24. VIOLATED
___ 25. PROLONGS

A. Scorn; disparaging or haughty disdain
B. Shaking or agitating violently with irregular and involuntary muscular contractions
C. To carry on through despite hardships
D. Calm; quiet
E. Gained as an objective; achieved
F. Producing a display of lustrous, rainbowlike colors
G. Something, esp. food, that sustains life or health
H. Not affected by a given influence; unresponsive
I. Characterized by or suggestive of doing good
J. Disfigured beyond repair
K. An animal that feeds on decaying matter
L. Emission of light without burning
M. Broke or disregarded
N. A seat across a boat on which a rower may sit
O. A light, sharp-pointed sword lacking a cutting edge and used only for thrusting
P. Unbearable
Q. Lowering the pride, dignity or self-respect
R. Gathered; assembled
S. Marked by meekness or modesty in behavior
T. Began; started
U. Something disposed to do evil; highly injurious
V. Firm determination
W. To lengthen in duration; protract
X. To form, plan, or arrange in one's mind; design or contrive
Y. Rolled up and secured to something

Old Man & The Sea Vocabulary Matching 4 Answer Key

X - 1. DEVISE
H - 2. IMMUNE
E - 3. ATTAINED
C - 4. ENDURES
Y - 5. FURLED
F - 6. IRIDESCENT
O - 7. RAPIER
V - 8. RESOLUTION
A - 9. CONTEMPT
T - 10. COMMENCED
D - 11. PLACID
J - 12. MUTILATED
G - 13. SUSTENANCE
S - 14. HUMILITY
I - 15. BENEVOLENT
N - 16. THWART
B - 17. CONVULSIVELY
L - 18. PHOSPHORESCENCE
P - 19. INTOLERABLE
Q - 20. HUMILIATING
K - 21. SCAVENGER
U - 22. MALIGNANCY
R - 23. CONGREGATED
M - 24. VIOLATED
W - 25. PROLONGS

A. Scorn; disparaging or haughty disdain
B. Shaking or agitating violently with irregular and involuntary muscular contractions
C. To carry on through despite hardships
D. Calm; quiet
E. Gained as an objective; achieved
F. Producing a display of lustrous, rainbowlike colors
G. Something, esp. food, that sustains life or health
H. Not affected by a given influence; unresponsive
I. Characterized by or suggestive of doing good
J. Disfigured beyond repair
K. An animal that feeds on decaying matter
L. Emission of light without burning
M. Broke or disregarded
N. A seat across a boat on which a rower may sit
O. A light, sharp-pointed sword lacking a cutting edge and used only for thrusting
P. Unbearable
Q. Lowering the pride, dignity or self-respect
R. Gathered; assembled
S. Marked by meekness or modesty in behavior
T. Began; started
U. Something disposed to do evil; highly injurious
V. Firm determination
W. To lengthen in duration; protract
X. To form, plan, or arrange in one's mind; design or contrive
Y. Rolled up and secured to something

Old Man & The Sea Vocabulary Magic Squares 1

Match the definition with the vocabulary word. Put your answers in the magic squares below. When your answers are correct, all columns and rows will add to the same number.

A. SCAVENGER
B. RAPIER
C. HUMILIATING
D. HUMILITY
E. DEVISE
F. VIOLATED
G. MALIGNANCY
H. INEFFECTUAL
I. IMMUNE
J. ATTAINED
K. IRIDESCENT
L. BENEVOLENT
M. CONTEMPT
N. FATHOMS
O. CONGREGATED
P. INTOLERABLE

1. Insufficient to produce a desired effect
2. Scorn; disparaging or haughty disdain
3. A light, sharp-pointed sword lacking a cutting edge and used only for thrusting
4. Producing a display of lustrous, rainbowlike colors
5. Gained as an objective; achieved
6. Lowering the pride, dignity or self-respect
7. Unbearable
8. To form, plan, or arrange in one's mind; design or contrive
9. Gathered; assembled
10. Broke or disregarded
11. Not affected by a given influence; unresponsive
12. Marked by meekness or modesty in behavior
13. An animal that feeds on decaying matter
14. Characterized by or suggestive of doing good
15. Something disposed to do evil; highly injurious
16. Units of length equal to six feet

A=	B=	C=	D=
E=	F=	G=	H=
I=	J=	K=	L=
M=	N=	O=	P=

Old Man & The Sea Vocabulary Magic Squares 1 Answer Key

Match the definition with the vocabulary word. Put your answers in the magic squares below. When your answers are correct, all columns and rows will add to the same number.

A. SCAVENGER
B. RAPIER
C. HUMILIATING
D. HUMILITY
E. DEVISE
F. VIOLATED
G. MALIGNANCY
H. INEFFECTUAL
I. IMMUNE
J. ATTAINED
K. IRIDESCENT
L. BENEVOLENT
M. CONTEMPT
N. FATHOMS
O. CONGREGATED
P. INTOLERABLE

1. Insufficient to produce a desired effect
2. Scorn; disparaging or haughty disdain
3. A light, sharp-pointed sword lacking a cutting edge and used only for thrusting
4. Producing a display of lustrous, rainbowlike colors
5. Gained as an objective; achieved
6. Lowering the pride, dignity or self-respect
7. Unbearable
8. To form, plan, or arrange in one's mind; design or contrive
9. Gathered; assembled
10. Broke or disregarded
11. Not affected by a given influence; unresponsive
12. Marked by meekness or modesty in behavior
13. An animal that feeds on decaying matter
14. Characterized by or suggestive of doing good
15. Something disposed to do evil; highly injurious
16. Units of length equal to six feet

A=13	B=3	C=6	D=12
E=8	F=10	G=15	H=1
I=11	J=5	K=4	L=14
M=2	N=16	O=9	P=7

Old Man & The Sea Vocabulary Magic Squares 2

Match the definition with the vocabulary word. Put your answers in the magic squares below. When your answers are correct, all columns and rows will add to the same number.

A. INEFFECTUAL
B. PROLONGS
C. CONVULSIVELY
D. CONGREGATED
E. COMMENCED
F. PLACID
G. IMMUNE
H. FATHOMS
I. RAPIER
J. MALIGNANCY
K. SCAVENGER
L. VIOLATED
M. RESOLUTION
N. HUMILITY
O. BENEVOLENT
P. HUMILIATING

1. Marked by meekness or modesty in behavior
2. Not affected by a given influence; unresponsive
3. Broke or disregarded
4. Insufficient to produce a desired effect
5. An animal that feeds on decaying matter
6. To lengthen in duration; protract
7. Firm determination
8. Units of length equal to six feet
9. Began; started
10. Lowering the pride, dignity or self-respect
11. Shaking or agitating violently with irregular and involuntary muscular contractions
12. Something disposed to do evil; highly injurious
13. Gathered; assembled
14. A light, sharp-pointed sword lacking a cutting edge and used only for thrusting
15. Calm; quiet
16. Characterized by or suggestive of doing good

A=	B=	C=	D=
E=	F=	G=	H=
I=	J=	K=	L=
M=	N=	O=	P=

Old Man & The Sea Vocabulary Magic Squares 2 Answer Key

Match the definition with the vocabulary word. Put your answers in the magic squares below. When your answers are correct, all columns and rows will add to the same number.

A. INEFFECTUAL
B. PROLONGS
C. CONVULSIVELY
D. CONGREGATED
E. COMMENCED
F. PLACID
G. IMMUNE
H. FATHOMS
I. RAPIER
J. MALIGNANCY
K. SCAVENGER
L. VIOLATED
M. RESOLUTION
N. HUMILITY
O. BENEVOLENT
P. HUMILIATING

1. Marked by meekness or modesty in behavior
2. Not affected by a given influence; unresponsive
3. Broke or disregarded
4. Insufficient to produce a desired effect
5. An animal that feeds on decaying matter
6. To lengthen in duration; protract
7. Firm determination
8. Units of length equal to six feet
9. Began; started
10. Lowering the pride, dignity or self-respect
11. Shaking or agitating violently with irregular and involuntary muscular contractions
12. Something disposed to do evil; highly injurious
13. Gathered; assembled
14. A light, sharp-pointed sword lacking a cutting edge and used only for thrusting
15. Calm; quiet
16. Characterized by or suggestive of doing good

A=4	B=6	C=11	D=13
E=9	F=15	G=2	H=8
I=14	J=12	K=5	L=3
M=7	N=1	O=16	P=10

Old Man & The Sea Vocabulary Magic Squares 3

Match the definition with the vocabulary word. Put your answers in the magic squares below. When your answers are correct, all columns and rows will add to the same number.

A. RESOLUTION
B. MALIGNANCY
C. INTOLERABLE
D. PLACID
E. PROLONGS
F. ATTAINED
G. IMMUNE
H. MUTILATED
I. CONTEMPT
J. CONVULSIVELY
K. FURLED
L. THWART
M. PHOSPHORESCENCE
N. HUMILITY
O. IRIDESCENT
P. FATHOMS

1. Marked by meekness or modesty in behavior
2. Not affected by a given influence; unresponsive
3. A seat across a boat on which a rower may sit
4. Firm determination
5. Rolled up and secured to something
6. Something disposed to do evil; highly injurious
7. Emission of light without burning
8. Disfigured beyond repair
9. To lengthen in duration; protract
10. Units of length equal to six feet
11. Unbearable
12. Shaking or agitating violently with irregular and involuntary muscular contractions
13. Calm; quiet
14. Scorn; disparaging or haughty disdain
15. Gained as an objective; achieved
16. Producing a display of lustrous, rainbowlike colors

A=	B=	C=	D=
E=	F=	G=	H=
I=	J=	K=	L=
M=	N=	O=	P=

Old Man & The Sea Vocabulary Magic Squares 3 Answer Key

Match the definition with the vocabulary word. Put your answers in the magic squares below. When your answers are correct, all columns and rows will add to the same number.

A. RESOLUTION
B. MALIGNANCY
C. INTOLERABLE
D. PLACID
E. PROLONGS
F. ATTAINED
G. IMMUNE
H. MUTILATED
I. CONTEMPT
J. CONVULSIVELY
K. FURLED
L. THWART
M. PHOSPHORESCENCE
N. HUMILITY
O. IRIDESCENT
P. FATHOMS

1. Marked by meekness or modesty in behavior
2. Not affected by a given influence; unresponsive
3. A seat across a boat on which a rower may sit
4. Firm determination
5. Rolled up and secured to something
6. Something disposed to do evil; highly injurious
7. Emission of light without burning
8. Disfigured beyond repair
9. To lengthen in duration; protract
10. Units of length equal to six feet
11. Unbearable
12. Shaking or agitating violently with irregular and involuntary muscular contractions
13. Calm; quiet
14. Scorn; disparaging or haughty disdain
15. Gained as an objective; achieved
16. Producing a display of lustrous, rainbowlike colors

A=4	B=6	C=11	D=13
E=9	F=15	G=2	H=8
I=14	J=12	K=5	L=3
M=7	N=1	O=16	P=10

Old Man & The Sea Vocabulary Magic Squares 4

Match the definition with the vocabulary word. Put your answers in the magic squares below. When your answers are correct, all columns and rows will add to the same number.

A. IMMUNE
B. MUTILATED
C. CONVULSIVELY
D. HUMILITY
E. MALIGNANCY
F. INTOLERABLE
G. PROLONGS
H. INEFFECTUAL
I. CONTEMPT
J. COMMENCED
K. DEVISE
L. VIOLATED
M. SUSTENANCE
N. RESOLUTION
O. HUMILIATING
P. RAPIER

1. Not affected by a given influence; unresponsive
2. Firm determination
3. Began; started
4. Something disposed to do evil; highly injurious
5. To lengthen in duration; protract
6. Broke or disregarded
7. A light, sharp-pointed sword lacking a cutting edge and used only for thrusting
8. Shaking or agitating violently with irregular and involuntary muscular contractions
9. Lowering the pride, dignity or self-respect
10. Marked by meekness or modesty in behavior
11. Insufficient to produce a desired effect
12. To form, plan, or arrange in one's mind; design or contrive
13. Scorn; disparaging or haughty disdain
14. Unbearable
15. Disfigured beyond repair
16. Something, esp. food, that sustains life or health

A=	B=	C=	D=
E=	F=	G=	H=
I=	J=	K=	L=
M=	N=	O=	P=

Old Man & The Sea Vocabulary Magic Squares 4 Answer Key

Match the definition with the vocabulary word. Put your answers in the magic squares below. When your answers are correct, all columns and rows will add to the same number.

A. IMMUNE
B. MUTILATED
C. CONVULSIVELY
D. HUMILITY
E. MALIGNANCY
F. INTOLERABLE
G. PROLONGS
H. INEFFECTUAL
I. CONTEMPT
J. COMMENCED
K. DEVISE
L. VIOLATED
M. SUSTENANCE
N. RESOLUTION
O. HUMILIATING
P. RAPIER

1. Not affected by a given influence; unresponsive
2. Firm determination
3. Began; started
4. Something disposed to do evil; highly injurious
5. To lengthen in duration; protract
6. Broke or disregarded
7. A light, sharp-pointed sword lacking a cutting edge and used only for thrusting
8. Shaking or agitating violently with irregular and involuntary muscular contractions
9. Lowering the pride, dignity or self-respect
10. Marked by meekness or modesty in behavior
11. Insufficient to produce a desired effect
12. To form, plan, or arrange in one's mind; design or contrive
13. Scorn; disparaging or haughty disdain
14. Unbearable
15. Disfigured beyond repair
16. Something, esp. food, that sustains life or health

A=1	B=15	C=8	D=10
E=4	F=14	G=5	H=11
I=13	J=3	K=12	L=6
M=16	N=2	O=9	P=7

Old Man & The Sea Vocabulary Word Search 1

Words are placed backwards, forward, diagonally, up and down. Clues listed below can help you find the words. Circle the hidden vocabulary words in the maze.

```
P N S C H U M I L I A T I N G L Q J I B
H K C O N G R E G A T E D Z P L W V N L
O B E N E V O L E N T P C C A Y C H T V
S R S V W X G G R H M V H U V P W H O G
P E V U D X H P E K V Q T W K H L U L B
H S T L S Y D N R T Z C F H Z X F M E R
O O S S D T D G L O E C R B W K X I R J
R L Z I W U E D M F L E D I J A Y L A T
E U D V R D D N F Y I O E X M L R I B Y
S T K E Y Z S E A P C O N T E M P T L J
C I S L V M N C A N D P I G B A U Y E F
E O D Y O I G R A T C M A K S L F N X Q
N N E H P F S Q W V C E T D Z I R P E Y
C Q T C U G C E B T E M T J Y G V L C D
E A A R K N Q H N Z C N A R J N D A R G
F K L N G K X L Y Z K H G H C A Y C N H
X E O C O M M E N C E D B E L N Q I Y F
D X I R I D E S C E N T Y B R C G D B Y
W K V M U T I L A T E D G C B Y G J J G
```

A light, sharp-pointed sword lacking a cutting edge and used only for thrusting (6)
A seat across a boat on which a rower may sit (6)
An animal that feeds on decaying matter (9)
Began; started (9)
Broke or disregarded (8)
Calm; quiet (6)
Characterized by or suggestive of doing good (10)
Disfigured beyond repair (9)
Emission of light without burning (15)
Firm determination (10)
Gained as an objective; achieved (8)
Gathered; assembled (11)
Insufficient to produce a desired effect (11)
Lowering the pride, dignity or self-respect (11)
Marked by meekness or modesty in behavior (8)
Not affected by a given influence; unresponsive (6)
Producing a display of lustrous, rainbowlike colors (10)
Rolled up and secured to something (6)
Scorn; disparaging or haughty disdain (8)
Shaking or agitating violently with irregular and involuntary muscular contractions (12)
Something disposed to do evil; highly injurious (10)
Something, esp. food, that sustains life or health (10)
To carry on through despite hardships (7)
To form, plan, or arrange in one's mind; design or contrive (6)
To lengthen in duration; protract (8)
Unbearable (11)
Units of length equal to six feet (7)

Old Man & The Sea Vocabulary Word Search 1 Answer Key

Words are placed backwards, forward, diagonally, up and down. Clues listed below can help you find the words. Circle the hidden vocabulary words in the maze.

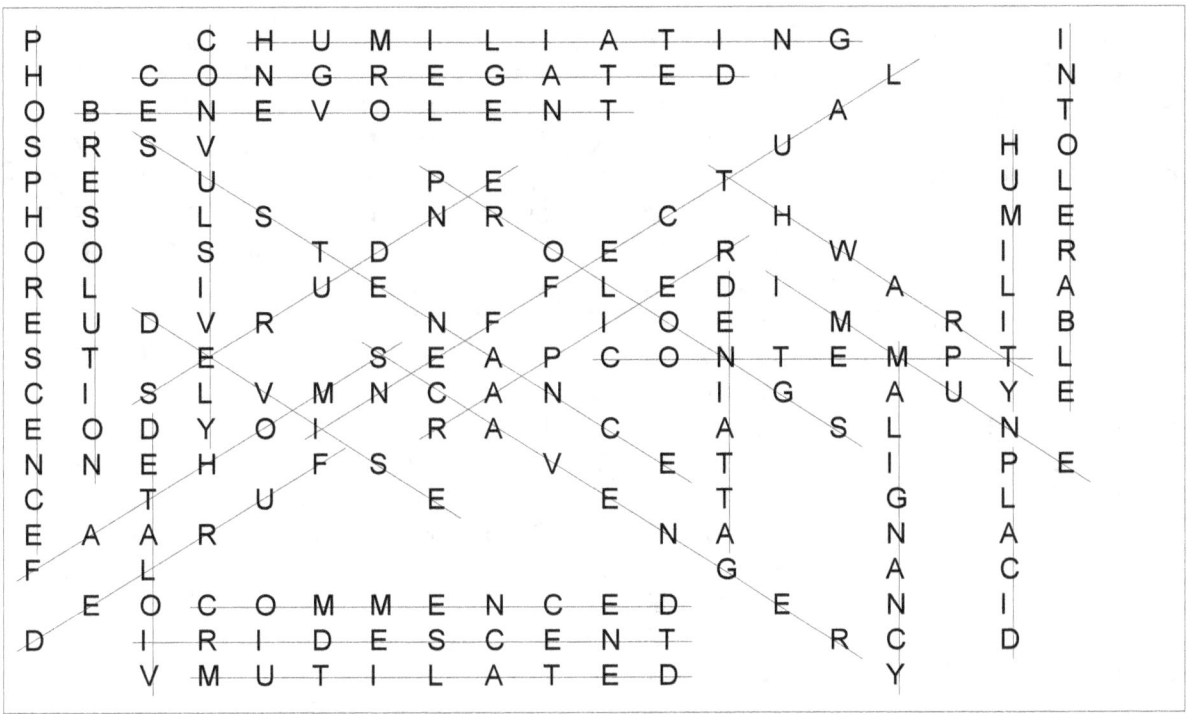

A light, sharp-pointed sword lacking a cutting edge and used only for thrusting (6)
A seat across a boat on which a rower may sit (6)
An animal that feeds on decaying matter (9)
Began; started (9)
Broke or disregarded (8)
Calm; quiet (6)
Characterized by or suggestive of doing good (10)
Disfigured beyond repair (9)
Emission of light without burning (15)
Firm determination (10)
Gained as an objective; achieved (8)
Gathered; assembled (11)
Insufficient to produce a desired effect (11)
Lowering the pride, dignity or self-respect (11)
Marked by meekness or modesty in behavior (8)
Not affected by a given influence; unresponsive (6)
Producing a display of lustrous, rainbowlike colors (10)
Rolled up and secured to something (6)
Scorn; disparaging or haughty disdain (8)
Shaking or agitating violently with irregular and involuntary muscular contractions (12)
Something disposed to do evil; highly injurious (10)
Something, esp. food, that sustains life or health (10)
To carry on through despite hardships (7)
To form, plan, or arrange in one's mind; design or contrive (6)
To lengthen in duration; protract (8)
Unbearable (11)
Units of length equal to six feet (7)

Old Man & The Sea Vocabulary Word Search 2

Words are placed backwards, forward, diagonally, up and down. Clues listed below can help you find the words. Circle the hidden vocabulary words in the maze.

```
T H W A R T H D E V I S E F R T S S Z H
N Q U X F Z U F Y Q Z C K E J A G R Z J
E R I M C S M B R L N N G H C N P M C I
L D R M I L I K K A K N K W O Q N I M W
O S I C G L L L N N E N H L N T K M E R
V T D L C T I E W V O Q O K G M U C W R
E W E H M J T A A I S R D S R N K C R C
N F S Y H S Y C T W P T P M E T N O C M
E C C S U Z S U O I N N K M G Y I Y S Q
B C E S Q Q L K Q M N V V Z A F N T F Z
Y F N R J O Y H R S M G Y F T P T F A K
H F T G S G Y W Y C A E P Q E L O V T B
S S C E D T Y T Y G T G N W D A L I H G
T P R Y K L S S M Z T Z D C J C E O O V
M A L I G N A N C Y A C S B E I R L M B
J V H L D C G M U T I L A T E D A A S Q
D L A U T C E F F E N I R D L B B T B C
V C O N V U L S I V E L Y J R N L E T K
E N D U R E S Q P S D E L R U F E D N Q
```

A light, sharp-pointed sword lacking a cutting edge and used only for thrusting (6)
A seat across a boat on which a rower may sit (6)
An animal that feeds on decaying matter (9)
Began; started (9)
Broke or disregarded (8)
Calm; quiet (6)
Characterized by or suggestive of doing good (10)
Disfigured beyond repair (9)
Firm determination (10)
Gained as an objective; achieved (8)
Gathered; assembled (11)
Insufficient to produce a desired effect (11)
Lowering the pride, dignity or self-respect (11)
Marked by meekness or modesty in behavior (8)
Not affected by a given influence; unresponsive (6)

Producing a display of lustrous, rainbowlike colors (10)
Rolled up and secured to something (6)
Scorn; disparaging or haughty disdain (8)
Shaking or agitating violently with irregular and involuntary muscular contractions (12)
Something disposed to do evil; highly injurious (10)
Something, esp. food, that sustains life or health (10)
To carry on through despite hardships (7)
To form, plan, or arrange in one's mind; design or contrive (6)
To lengthen in duration; protract (8)
Unbearable (11)
Units of length equal to six feet (7)

Old Man & The Sea Vocabulary Word Search 2 Answer Key

Words are placed backwards, forward, diagonally, up and down. Clues listed below can help you find the words. Circle the hidden vocabulary words in the maze.

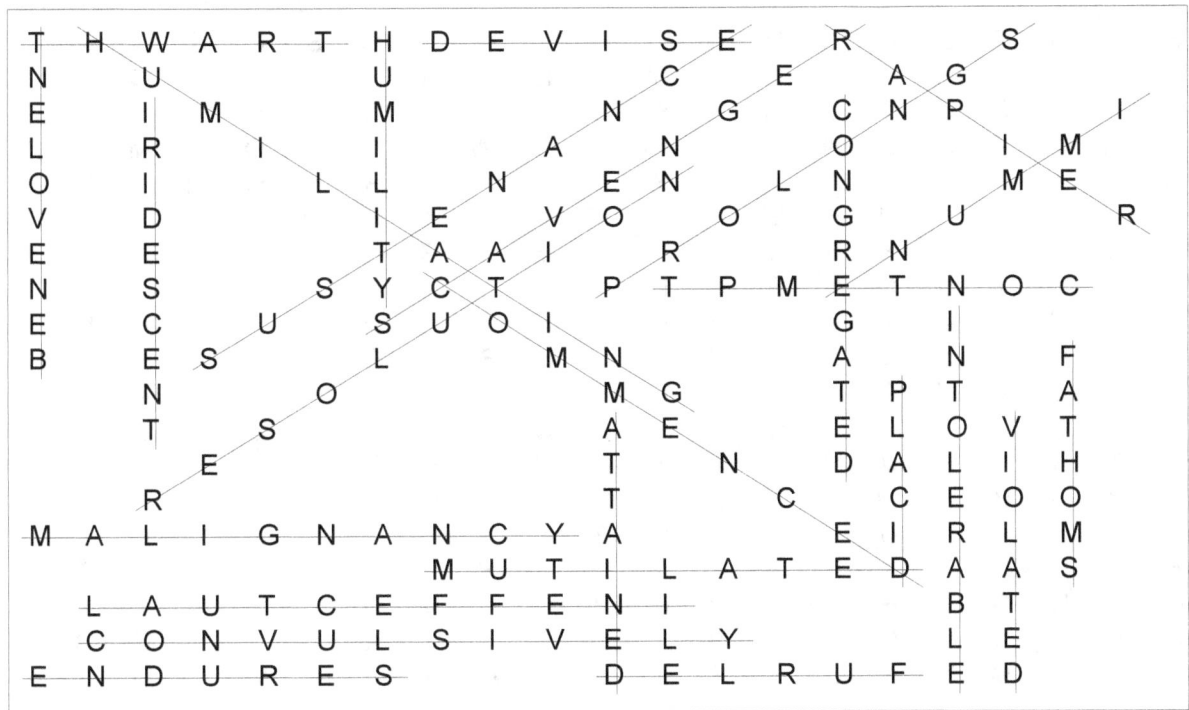

A light, sharp-pointed sword lacking a cutting edge and used only for thrusting (6)
A seat across a boat on which a rower may sit (6)
An animal that feeds on decaying matter (9)
Began; started (9)
Broke or disregarded (8)
Calm; quiet (6)
Characterized by or suggestive of doing good (10)
Disfigured beyond repair (9)
Firm determination (10)
Gained as an objective; achieved (8)
Gathered; assembled (11)
Insufficient to produce a desired effect (11)
Lowering the pride, dignity or self-respect (11)
Marked by meekness or modesty in behavior (8)
Not affected by a given influence; unresponsive (6)
Producing a display of lustrous, rainbowlike colors (10)
Rolled up and secured to something (6)
Scorn; disparaging or haughty disdain (8)
Shaking or agitating violently with irregular and involuntary muscular contractions (12)
Something disposed to do evil; highly injurious (10)
Something, esp. food, that sustains life or health (10)
To carry on through despite hardships (7)
To form, plan, or arrange in one's mind; design or contrive (6)
To lengthen in duration; protract (8)
Unbearable (11)
Units of length equal to six feet (7)

Old Man & The Sea Vocabulary Word Search 3

Words are placed backwards, forward, diagonally, up and down. Words listed below are included in the maze. Circle the hidden vocabulary words in the maze.

```
S U S T E N A N C E I R I D E S C E N T
T C S D H J Y H U M I L I A T I N G C P
E T A G S F C Q N P C N Z F E X B C D F
C W V V D S N Y F W O Z W S Y Q Q V M N
N J Z B E N A F D Y M W I Z R G I M J P
E I J Y R N N S R D M V Z X P O L W T D
C N R F E R G L Y L E V I S L U V N O C
S T N Y S N I E X D N L H A R Z E D G T
E O G P O W L D R H C S T G P L G D R D
R L P L L M A A M Z E E S M O H T A F F
O E O Z U A M G T B D V B V V P W L M X
H R G J T I C C S T E Q E R M H Z C U P
P A K V I M W I X N A N E E T U P Y T M
S B S B O M F N D J E I T F G M Y V I P
O L S R N U G U E B P N N C G I D V L T
H E R D C N R R L A O Y H E Q L K S A Z
P C K G S E R C R C P G Y M D I S G T X
F H C B S M L V U V J J Y P X T L Y E D
T L L M I N E F F E C T U A L Y W C D Q
```

ATTAINED   HUMILIATING   PLACID

BENEVOLENT   HUMILITY   PROLONGS

COMMENCED   IMMUNE   RAPIER

CONTEMPT   INEFFECTUAL   RESOLUTION

CONVULSIVELY   INTOLERABLE   SCAVENGER

DEVISE   IRIDESCENT   SUSTENANCE

ENDURES   MALIGNANCY   THWART

FATHOMS   MUTILATED   VIOLATED

FURLED   PHOSPHORESCENCE

Old Man & The Sea Vocabulary Word Search 3 Answer Key

Words are placed backwards, forward, diagonally, up and down. Words listed below are included in the maze. Circle the hidden vocabulary words in the maze.

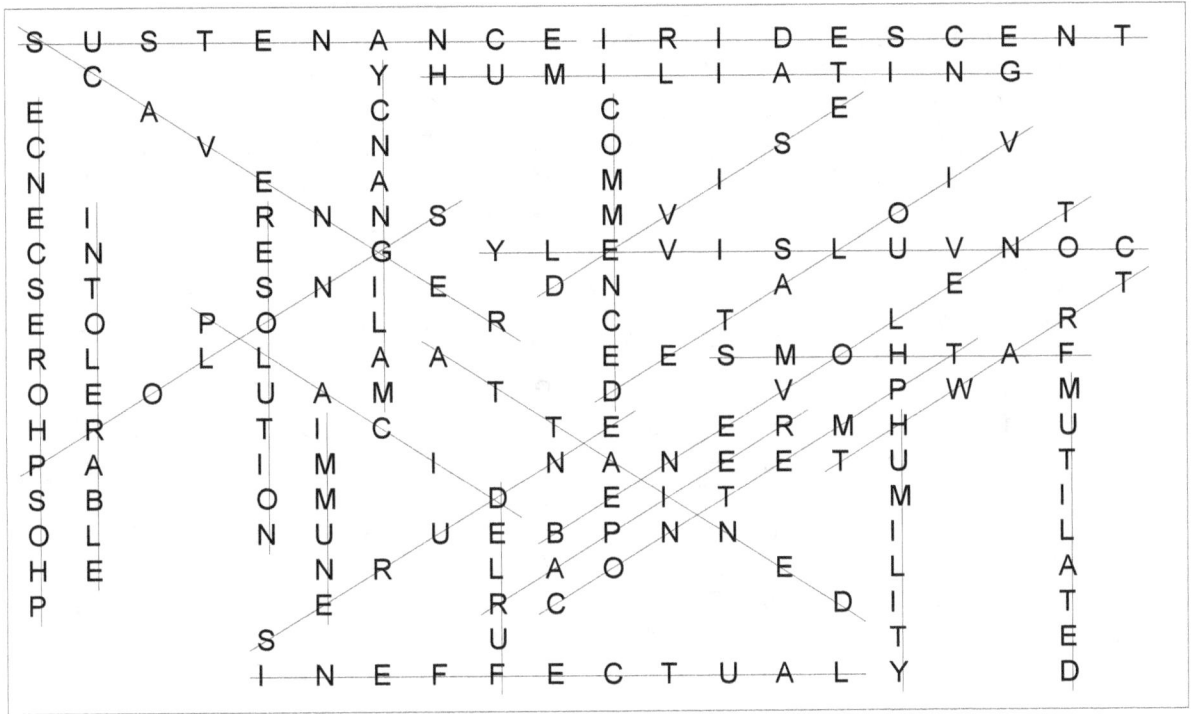

ATTAINED	HUMILIATING	PLACID
BENEVOLENT	HUMILITY	PROLONGS
COMMENCED	IMMUNE	RAPIER
CONTEMPT	INEFFECTUAL	RESOLUTION
CONVULSIVELY	INTOLERABLE	SCAVENGER
DEVISE	IRIDESCENT	SUSTENANCE
ENDURES	MALIGNANCY	THWART
FATHOMS	MUTILATED	VIOLATED
FURLED	PHOSPHORESCENCE	

Old Man & The Sea Vocabulary Word Search 4

Words are placed backwards, forward, diagonally, up and down. Words listed below are included in the maze. Circle the hidden vocabulary words in the maze.

```
I  N  T  O  L  E  R  A  B  L  E  P  X  Z  L  B  C  S  Y  X
C  O  N  V  U  L  S  I  V  E  L  Y  G  D  E  P  G  U  C  B
X  J  L  A  U  T  C  E  F  F  E  N  I  N  P  P  H  S  H  Z
R  G  D  N  W  M  F  R  I  R  I  D  E  S  C  E  N  T  D  S
P  R  O  L  O  N  G  S  E  T  Q  V  M  V  F  R  P  E  V  Y
L  K  B  V  K  R  F  M  A  S  O  G  K  F  Y  D  L  N  P  T
V  J  Z  P  K  Z  L  I  U  L  O  J  E  T  U  D  F  A  L  R
I  L  L  K  H  H  L  H  E  T  D  L  I  N  D  R  G  N  A  S
C  M  G  Z  M  I  A  N  D  G  I  L  U  L  D  E  L  C  C  V
O  S  M  N  M  M  T  E  S  L  I  L  M  T  J  U  V  E  I  W
N  G  X  U  F  A  T  H  O  M  S  R  A  P  I  E  R  I  D  T
G  N  H  M  N  A  A  H  U  C  C  G  L  T  S  O  N  E  S  Y
R  M  S  R  L  E  I  H  A  M  O  L  I  T  E  H  N  K  S  E
E  F  H  O  R  W  N  V  W  J  N  C  G  S  Z  D  S  S  C  Z
G  J  I  D  P  F  E  V  H  J  T  X  N  F  S  N  Z  G  R  K
A  V  W  B  K  N  D  G  J  R  E  P  A  N  J  W  W  P  Q  K
T  Q  F  D  G  P  B  C  O  M  M  E  N  C  E  D  R  G  R  Q
E  L  V  E  M  P  D  J  L  M  P  X  C  Q  N  J  T  M  S  H
D  N  R  P  S  T  H  W  A  R  T  Q  Y  C  J  Q  S  P  X  N
```

ATTAINED	FURLED	PLACID
BENEVOLENT	HUMILIATING	PROLONGS
COMMENCED	HUMILITY	RAPIER
CONGREGATED	IMMUNE	RESOLUTION
CONTEMPT	INEFFECTUAL	SCAVENGER
CONVULSIVELY	INTOLERABLE	SUSTENANCE
DEVISE	IRIDESCENT	THWART
ENDURES	MALIGNANCY	VIOLATED
FATHOMS	MUTILATED	

Old Man & The Sea Vocabulary Word Search 4 Answer Key

Words are placed backwards, forward, diagonally, up and down. Words listed below are included in the maze. Circle the hidden vocabulary words in the maze.

ATTAINED	FURLED	PLACID
BENEVOLENT	HUMILIATING	PROLONGS
COMMENCED	HUMILITY	RAPIER
CONGREGATED	IMMUNE	RESOLUTION
CONTEMPT	INEFFECTUAL	SCAVENGER
CONVULSIVELY	INTOLERABLE	SUSTENANCE
DEVISE	IRIDESCENT	THWART
ENDURES	MALIGNANCY	VIOLATED
FATHOMS	MUTILATED	

Old Man & The Sea Vocabulary Crossword 1

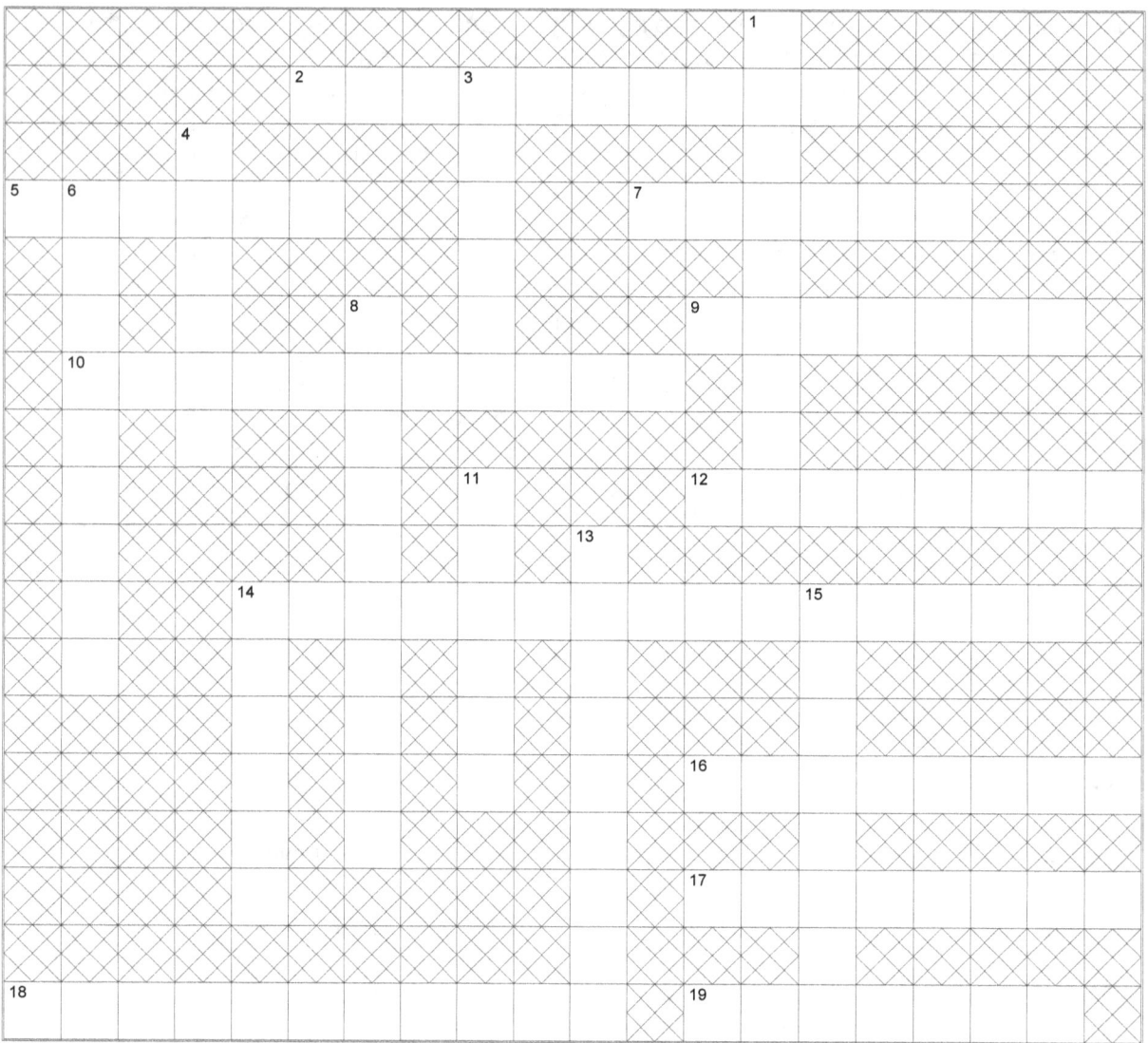

Across
2. Something, esp. food, that sustains life or health
5. Not affected by a given influence; unresponsive
7. To form, plan, or arrange in one's mind; design or contrive
9. To carry on through despite hardships
10. Insufficient to produce a desired effect
12. To lengthen in duration; protract
14. Emission of light without burning
16. Gained as an objective; achieved
17. Marked by meekness or modesty in behavior
18. Gathered; assembled
19. Units of length equal to six feet

Down
1. An animal that feeds on decaying matter
3. A seat across a boat on which a rower may sit
4. Rolled up and secured to something
6. Disfigured beyond repair
8. Characterized by or suggestive of doing good
11. A light, sharp-pointed sword lacking a cutting edge and used only for thrusting
13. Began; started
14. Calm; quiet
15. Scorn; disparaging or haughty disdain

Old Man & The Sea Vocabulary Crossword 1 Answer Key

											¹S			
			²S	U	S	³T	E	N	A	N	C	E		
		⁴F				H					A			
⁵I	⁶M	M	U	N	E		W		⁷D	E	V	I	S	E
	U		R				A				E			
	T		L		⁸B		R		⁹E	N	D	U	R	E	S
	¹⁰I	N	E	F	F	E	C	T	U	A	L			
	L		D		N				G					
	A				E		¹¹R		¹²P	R	O	L	O	N	G	S
	T				V		A		¹³C					
	E		¹⁴P	H	O	S	P	H	O	R	E	S	¹⁵C	E	N	C	E
	D		L		L		I		M				O		
			A		E		E		M				N		
			C		N		R		E			¹⁶A	T	T	A	I	N	E	D
			I		T				N				E		
			D						C		¹⁷H	U	M	I	L	I	T	Y
									E				P		
¹⁸C	O	N	G	R	E	G	A	T	E	D		¹⁹F	A	T	H	O	M	S

Across

2. Something, esp. food, that sustains life or health
5. Not affected by a given influence; unresponsive
7. To form, plan, or arrange in one's mind; design or contrive
9. To carry on through despite hardships
10. Insufficient to produce a desired effect
12. To lengthen in duration; protract
14. Emission of light without burning
16. Gained as an objective; achieved
17. Marked by meekness or modesty in behavior
18. Gathered; assembled
19. Units of length equal to six feet

Down

1. An animal that feeds on decaying matter
3. A seat across a boat on which a rower may sit
4. Rolled up and secured to something
6. Disfigured beyond repair
8. Characterized by or suggestive of doing good
11. A light, sharp-pointed sword lacking a cutting edge and used only for thrusting
13. Began; started
14. Calm; quiet
15. Scorn; disparaging or haughty disdain

Old Man & The Sea Vocabulary Crossword 2

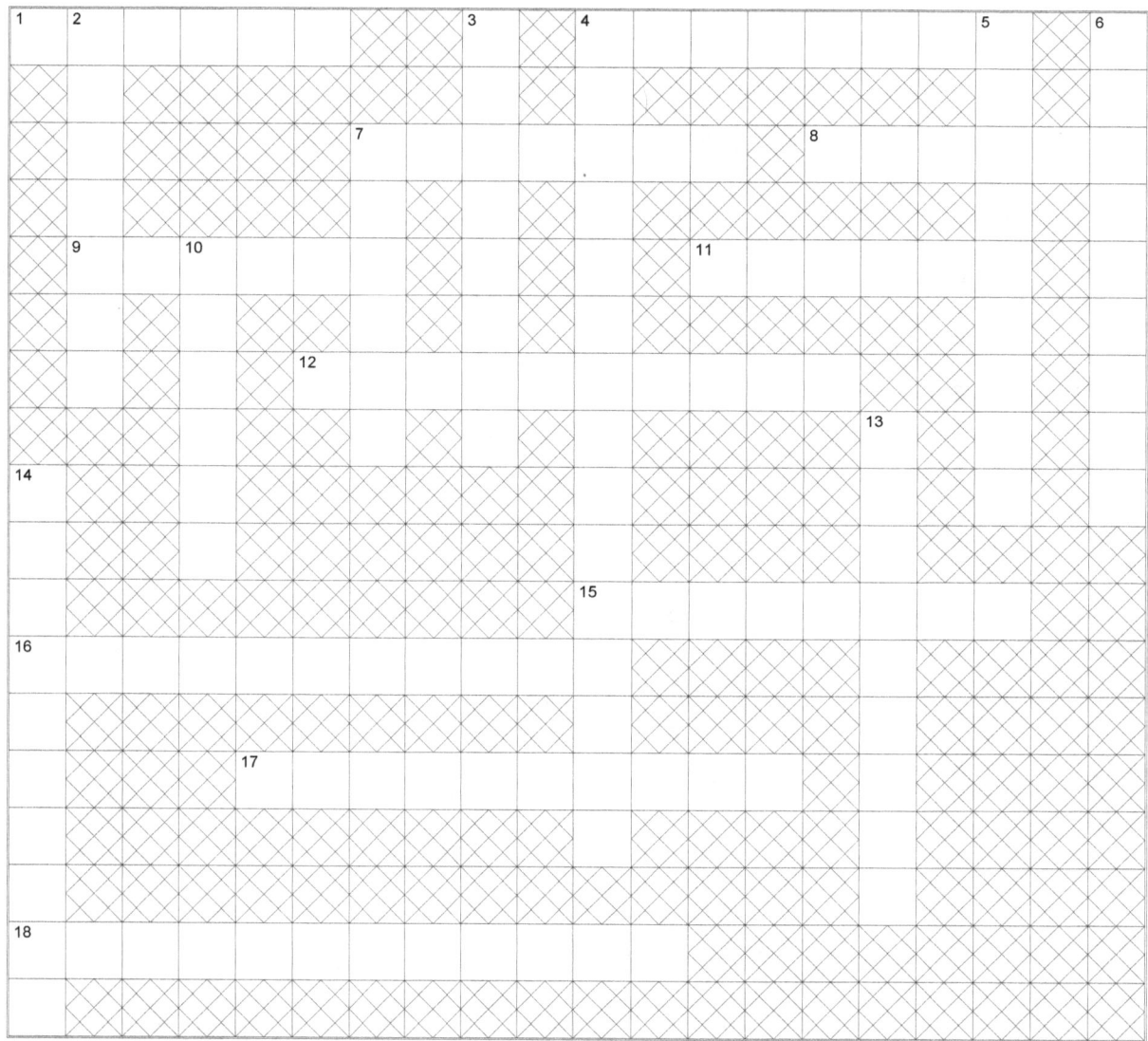

Across
1. To form, plan, or arrange in one's mind; design or contrive
4. To lengthen in duration; protract
7. Units of length equal to six feet
8. A seat across a boat on which a rower may sit
9. A light, sharp-pointed sword lacking a cutting edge and used only for thrusting
11. Not affected by a given influence; unresponsive
12. Characterized by or suggestive of doing good
15. Scorn; disparaging or haughty disdain
16. Unbearable
17. Producing a display of lustrous, rainbowlike colors
18. Shaking or agitating violently with irregular and involuntary muscular contractions

Down
2. To carry on through despite hardships
3. Gained as an objective; achieved
4. Emission of light without burning
5. An animal that feeds on decaying matter
6. Disfigured beyond repair
7. Rolled up and secured to something
10. Calm; quiet
13. Began; started
14. Something disposed to do evil; highly injurious

Old Man & The Sea Vocabulary Crossword 2 Answer Key

	1 D	2 E	V	I	S	E		3 A		4 P	R	O	L	O	N	G	S	5 S		6 M
		N						T		H								C		U
		D				7 F	A	T	H	O	M	S		8 T	H	W	A	R	T
		U				U		A		S								V		I
		9 R	A	10 P	I	E	R		I		P		11 I	M	M	U	N	E		L
		E		L					L		N							N		A
		S		A		12 B	E	N	E	V	O	L	E	N	T			G		T
				C					D		R						13 C		E	E
14 M				I					D		E						O		R	D
A				D							S						M			
L											15 C	O	N	T	E	M	P	T		
16 I	N	T	O	L	E	R	A	B	L	E							E			
G										N							N			
N				17 I	R	I	D	E	S	C	E	N	T				C			
A										E							E			
N																	D			
18 C	O	N	V	U	L	S	I	V	E	L	Y									
Y																				

Across
1. To form, plan, or arrange in one's mind; design or contrive
4. To lengthen in duration; protract
7. Units of length equal to six feet
8. A seat across a boat on which a rower may sit
9. A light, sharp-pointed sword lacking a cutting edge and used only for thrusting
11. Not affected by a given influence; unresponsive
12. Characterized by or suggestive of doing good
15. Scorn; disparaging or haughty disdain
16. Unbearable
17. Producing a display of lustrous, rainbowlike colors
18. Shaking or agitating violently with irregular and involuntary muscular contractions

Down
2. To carry on through despite hardships
3. Gained as an objective; achieved
4. Emission of light without burning
5. An animal that feeds on decaying matter
6. Disfigured beyond repair
7. Rolled up and secured to something
10. Calm; quiet
13. Began; started
14. Something disposed to do evil; highly injurious

Old Man & The Sea Vocabulary Crossword 3

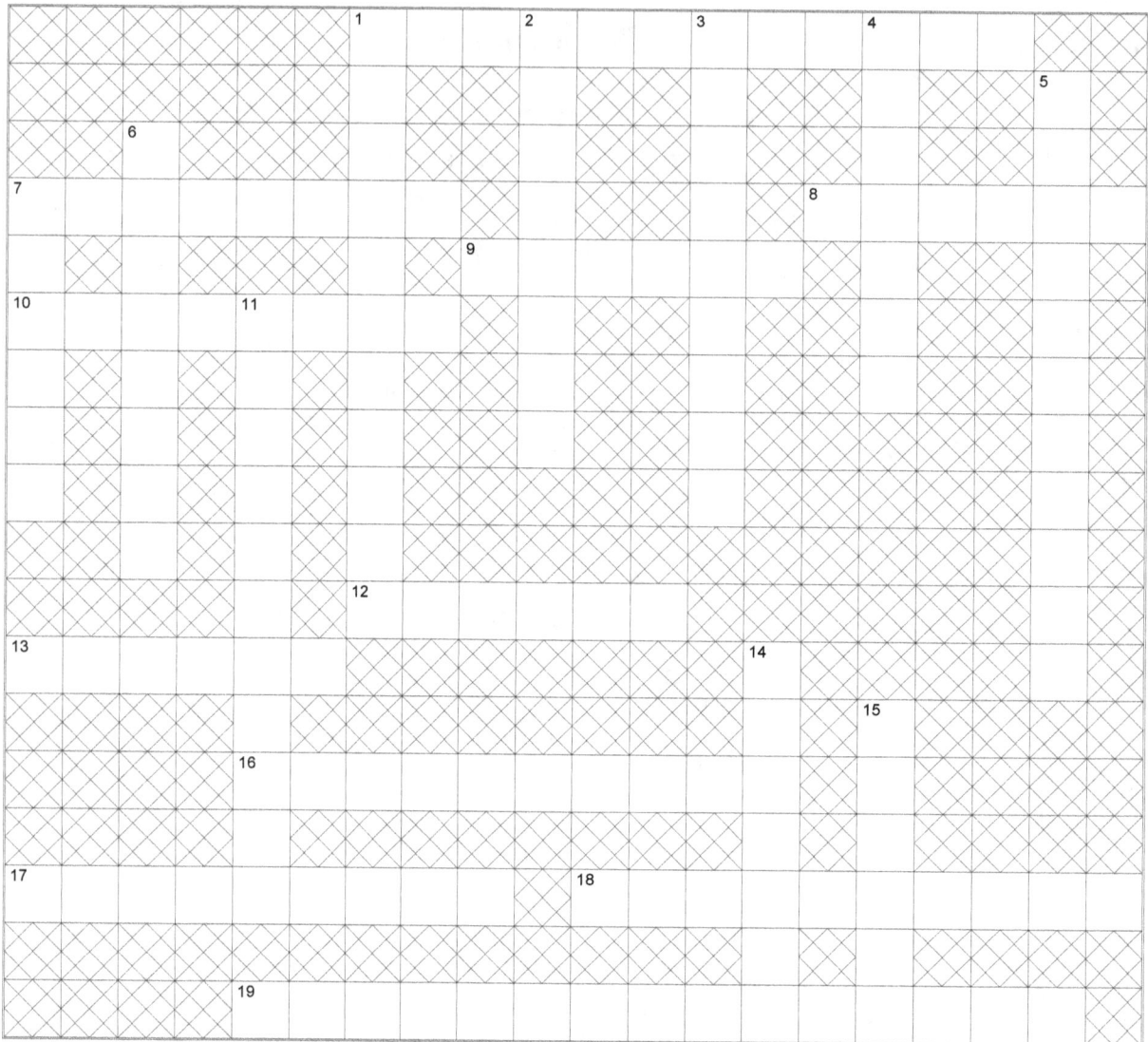

Across
1. Shaking or agitating violently with irregular and involuntary muscular contractions
7. To lengthen in duration; protract
8. Rolled up and secured to something
9. A light, sharp-pointed sword lacking a cutting edge and used only for thrusting
10. Gained as an objective; achieved
12. To form, plan, or arrange in one's mind; design or contrive
13. A seat across a boat on which a rower may sit
16. Characterized by or suggestive of doing good
17. Began; started
18. Firm determination
19. Emission of light without burning

Down
1. Gathered; assembled
2. Broke or disregarded
3. An animal that feeds on decaying matter
4. To carry on through despite hardships
5. Insufficient to produce a desired effect
6. Scorn; disparaging or haughty disdain
7. Calm; quiet
11. Unbearable
14. Units of length equal to six feet
15. Not affected by a given influence; unresponsive

Old Man & The Sea Vocabulary Crossword 3 Answer Key

Across grid solution:
- 1 Across: CONVULSIVELY
- 7 Across: PROLONGS
- 8 Across: FURLED
- 9 Across: RAPIER
- 10 Across: ATTAINED
- 12 Across: DEVISE
- 13 Across: THWART
- 16 Across: BENEVOLENT
- 17 Across: COMMENCED
- 18 Across: RESOLUTION
- 19 Across: PHOSPHORESCENCE

Down:
- 1 Down: CONGREGATED
- 2 Down: VIOLATED
- 3 Down: SCAVENGER
- 4 Down: ENDURE
- 5 Down: INEFFECTUAL
- 6 Down: CONTEMPT
- 7 Down: PLACID
- 11 Down: INTOLERABLE
- 14 Down: FATHOMS
- 15 Down: IMMUNE

Across
1. Shaking or agitating violently with irregular and involuntary muscular contractions
7. To lengthen in duration; protract
8. Rolled up and secured to something
9. A light, sharp-pointed sword lacking a cutting edge and used only for thrusting
10. Gained as an objective; achieved
12. To form, plan, or arrange in one's mind; design or contrive
13. A seat across a boat on which a rower may sit
16. Characterized by or suggestive of doing good
17. Began; started
18. Firm determination
19. Emission of light without burning

Down
1. Gathered; assembled
2. Broke or disregarded
3. An animal that feeds on decaying matter
4. To carry on through despite hardships
5. Insufficient to produce a desired effect
6. Scorn; disparaging or haughty disdain
7. Calm; quiet
11. Unbearable
14. Units of length equal to six feet
15. Not affected by a given influence; unresponsive

Old Man & The Sea Vocabulary Crossword 4

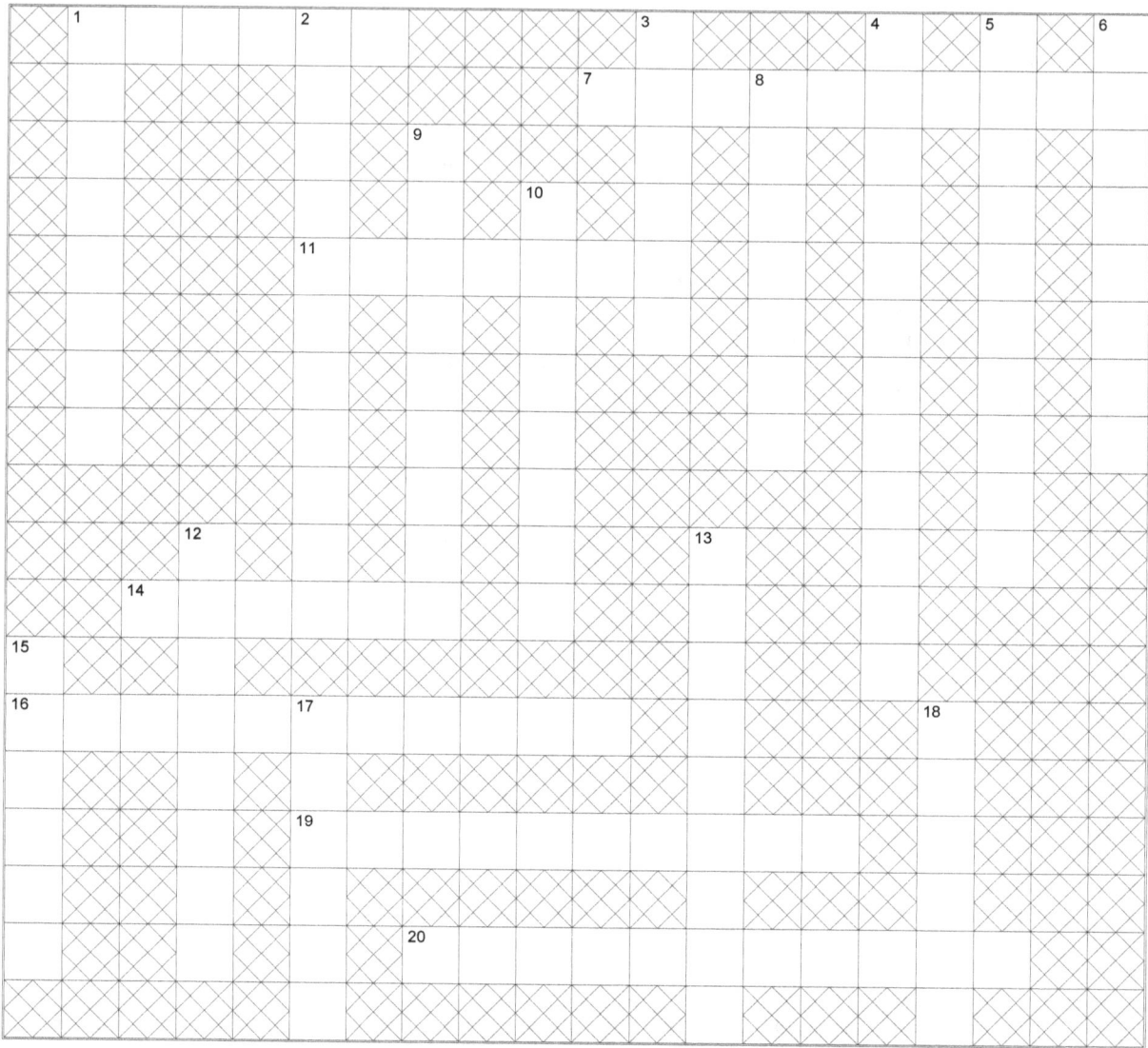

Across
1. Calm; quiet
7. Characterized by or suggestive of doing good
11. Units of length equal to six feet
14. Rolled up and secured to something
16. Lowering the pride, dignity or self-respect
19. Something disposed to do evil; highly injurious
20. Gathered; assembled

Down
1. To lengthen in duration; protract
2. Insufficient to produce a desired effect
3. To form, plan, or arrange in one's mind; design or contrive
4. Shaking or agitating violently with irregular and involuntary muscular contractions
5. Firm determination
6. Gained as an objective; achieved
8. To carry on through despite hardships
9. Disfigured beyond repair
10. Scorn; disparaging or haughty disdain
12. Marked by meekness or modesty in behavior
13. Began; started
15. A seat across a boat on which a rower may sit
17. Not affected by a given influence; unresponsive
18. A light, sharp-pointed sword lacking a cutting edge and used only for thrusting

Old Man & The Sea Vocabulary Crossword 4 Answer Key

	1 P	L	A	2 I	D			3 D		4 C		5 R		6 A
	R			N			7 B	E	8 E	V	O	L	E	N	T
	O			E		9 M		V		N		N		S		T
	L			F		U		10 C		I		D		V		O		A
	O			11 F	A	T	H	O	M	S		U		U		L		I
	N			E		I		N		E		R		L		U		N
	G			C		L		T				E		S		T		E
	S			T		A		E				S		I		I		D
				U		T		M						V		O		
			12 H	A		E		P		13 C			E		N		
			14 F	U	R	L	E	D		T		O			L			
15 T			M							M			Y		
16 H	U	M	I	17 L	I	A	T	I	N	G		M		18 R
W				L		M						E				A
A				I		19 M	A	L	I	G	N	A	N	C	Y		P
R				T		U						C				I
T				Y		N		20 C	O	N	G	R	E	G	A	T	E	D
						E						D				R

Across
1. Calm; quiet
7. Characterized by or suggestive of doing good
11. Units of length equal to six feet
14. Rolled up and secured to something
16. Lowering the pride, dignity or self-respect
19. Something disposed to do evil; highly injurious
20. Gathered; assembled

Down
1. To lengthen in duration; protract
2. Insufficient to produce a desired effect
3. To form, plan, or arrange in one's mind; design or contrive
4. Shaking or agitating violently with irregular and involuntary muscular contractions
5. Firm determination
6. Gained as an objective; achieved
8. To carry on through despite hardships
9. Disfigured beyond repair
10. Scorn; disparaging or haughty disdain
12. Marked by meekness or modesty in behavior
13. Began; started
15. A seat across a boat on which a rower may sit
17. Not affected by a given influence; unresponsive
18. A light, sharp-pointed sword lacking a cutting edge and used only for thrusting

Old Man & The Sea Vocabulary Juggle Letters 1

1. FAETINFUCLE = 1. _____
   Insufficient to produce a desired effect

2. OEMNCPTT = 2. _____
   Scorn; disparaging or haughty disdain

3. TIEADANT = 3. _____
   Gained as an objective; achieved

4. NNSUECEAST = 4. _____
   Something, esp. food, that sustains life or health

5. NUEESDR = 5. _____
   To carry on through despite hardships

6. OELBLANREIT = 6. _____
   Unbearable

7. AEOCDGTEGNR = 7. _____
   Gathered; assembled

8. RNCEAGVSE = 8. _____
   An animal that feeds on decaying matter

9. DEUTMIALT = 9. _____
   Disfigured beyond repair

10. TEONBNELEV =10. _____
    Characterized by or suggestive of doing good

11. TSNELROUIO =11. _____
    Firm determination

12. RWHATT =12. _____
    A seat across a boat on which a rower may sit

13. ICADPL =13. _____
    Calm; quiet

14. CEPCSORESEOPNHH =14. _____
    Emission of light without burning

15. TEIDSNEIRC =15. _____
    Producing a display of lustrous, rainbowlike colors

Old Man & The Sea Vocabulary Juggle Letters 1 Answer Key

1. FAETINFUCLE = 1. INEFFECTUAL
   Insufficient to produce a desired effect

2. OEMNCPTT = 2. CONTEMPT
   Scorn; disparaging or haughty disdain

3. TIEADANT = 3. ATTAINED
   Gained as an objective; achieved

4. NNSUECEAST = 4. SUSTENANCE
   Something, esp. food, that sustains life or health

5. NUEESDR = 5. ENDURES
   To carry on through despite hardships

6. OELBLANREIT = 6. INTOLERABLE
   Unbearable

7. AEOCDGTEGNR = 7. CONGREGATED
   Gathered; assembled

8. RNCEAGVSE = 8. SCAVENGER
   An animal that feeds on decaying matter

9. DEUTMIALT = 9. MUTILATED
   Disfigured beyond repair

10. TEONBNELEV =10. BENEVOLENT
    Characterized by or suggestive of doing good

11. TSNELROUIO =11. RESOLUTION
    Firm determination

12. RWHATT =12. THWART
    A seat across a boat on which a rower may sit

13. ICADPL =13. PLACID
    Calm; quiet

14. CEPCSORESEOPNHH =14. PHOSPHORESCENCE
    Emission of light without burning

15. TEIDSNEIRC =15. IRIDESCENT
    Producing a display of lustrous, rainbowlike colors

Old Man & The Sea Vocabulary Juggle Letters 2

1. ILCNYMANGA = 1. _____
   Something disposed to do evil; highly injurious

2. EOBATRNLELI = 2. _____
   Unbearable

3. VCESANEGR = 3. _____
   An animal that feeds on decaying matter

4. LFEUTACIFNE = 4. _____
   Insufficient to produce a desired effect

5. SCESEHEHPPNOROC = 5. _____
   Emission of light without burning

6. TIIEESNRDC = 6. _____
   Producing a display of lustrous, rainbowlike colors

7. ISEEVD = 7. _____
   To form, plan, or arrange in one's mind; design or contrive

8. HSMOTAF = 8. _____
   Units of length equal to six feet

9. NAEDTAIT = 9. _____
   Gained as an objective; achieved

10. NBNEEVLTEO = 10. _____
    Characterized by or suggestive of doing good

11. GSOOLNRP = 11. _____
    To lengthen in duration; protract

12. ETONTPCM = 12. _____
    Scorn; disparaging or haughty disdain

13. ATNORGCEDEG = 13. _____
    Gathered; assembled

14. WTATHR = 14. _____
    A seat across a boat on which a rower may sit

15. UIMENM = 15. _____
    Not affected by a given influence; unresponsive

Old Man & The Sea Vocabulary Juggle Letters 2 Answer Key

1. ILCNYMANGA = 1. MALIGNANCY
Something disposed to do evil; highly injurious

2. EOBATRNLELI = 2. INTOLERABLE
Unbearable

3. VCESANEGR = 3. SCAVENGER
An animal that feeds on decaying matter

4. LFEUTACIFNE = 4. INEFFECTUAL
Insufficient to produce a desired effect

5. SCESEHEHPPNOROC = 5. PHOSPHORESCENCE
Emission of light without burning

6. TIIEESNRDC = 6. IRIDESCENT
Producing a display of lustrous, rainbowlike colors

7. ISEEVD = 7. DEVISE
To form, plan, or arrange in one's mind; design or contrive

8. HSMOTAF = 8. FATHOMS
Units of length equal to six feet

9. NAEDTAIT = 9. ATTAINED
Gained as an objective; achieved

10. NBNEEVLTEO =10. BENEVOLENT
Characterized by or suggestive of doing good

11. GSOOLNRP =11. PROLONGS
To lengthen in duration; protract

12. ETONTPCM =12. CONTEMPT
Scorn; disparaging or haughty disdain

13. ATNORGCEDEG =13. CONGREGATED
Gathered; assembled

14. WTATHR =14. THWART
A seat across a boat on which a rower may sit

15. UIMENM =15. IMMUNE
Not affected by a given influence; unresponsive

Copyrighted

Old Man & The Sea Vocabulary Juggle Letters 3

1. OLVTAIED = 1. _____
   Broke or disregarded

2. TADIMEUTL = 2. _____
   Disfigured beyond repair

3. YLIHUTIM = 3. _____
   Marked by meekness or modesty in behavior

4. NDEIATAT = 4. _____
   Gained as an objective; achieved

5. RSLOOGNP = 5. _____
   To lengthen in duration; protract

6. MOFHATS = 6. _____
   Units of length equal to six feet

7. UCENSTSNAE = 7. _____
   Something, esp. food, that sustains life or health

8. VEELNENOBT = 8. _____
   Characterized by or suggestive of doing good

9. RSEEDUN = 9. _____
   To carry on through despite hardships

10. ECRISIDENT =10. _____
    Producing a display of lustrous, rainbowlike colors

11. NNIAGYLCMA =11. _____
    Something disposed to do evil; highly injurious

12. LEAORENTIBL =12. _____
    Unbearable

13. ACPLID =13. _____
    Calm; quiet

14. TWRHTA =14. _____
    A seat across a boat on which a rower may sit

15. ERANVECGS =15. _____
    An animal that feeds on decaying matter

Old Man & The Sea Vocabulary Juggle Letters 3 Answer Key

1. OLVTAIED = 1. VIOLATED
Broke or disregarded

2. TADIMEUTL = 2. MUTILATED
Disfigured beyond repair

3. YLIHUTIM = 3. HUMILITY
Marked by meekness or modesty in behavior

4. NDEIATAT = 4. ATTAINED
Gained as an objective; achieved

5. RSLOOGNP = 5. PROLONGS
To lengthen in duration; protract

6. MOFHATS = 6. FATHOMS
Units of length equal to six feet

7. UCENSTSNAE = 7. SUSTENANCE
Something, esp. food, that sustains life or health

8. VEELNENOBT = 8. BENEVOLENT
Characterized by or suggestive of doing good

9. RSEEDUN = 9. ENDURES
To carry on through despite hardships

10. ECRISIDENT = 10. IRIDESCENT
Producing a display of lustrous, rainbowlike colors

11. NNIAGYLCMA = 11. MALIGNANCY
Something disposed to do evil; highly injurious

12. LEAORENTIBL = 12. INTOLERABLE
Unbearable

13. ACPLID = 13. PLACID
Calm; quiet

14. TWRHTA = 14. THWART
A seat across a boat on which a rower may sit

15. ERANVECGS = 15. SCAVENGER
An animal that feeds on decaying matter

Old Man & The Sea Vocabulary Juggle Letters 4

1. EDFLRU = 1. _____
Rolled up and secured to something

2. SDEEIV = 2. _____
To form, plan, or arrange in one's mind; design or contrive

3. OLSIEROTUN = 3. _____
Firm determination

4. VEEACSNRG = 4. _____
An animal that feeds on decaying matter

5. NSEUEDR = 5. _____
To carry on through despite hardships

6. SIDECRITEN = 6. _____
Producing a display of lustrous, rainbowlike colors

7. CPHOOEHPEESCRNS = 7. _____
Emission of light without burning

8. TTPMEONC = 8. _____
Scorn; disparaging or haughty disdain

9. IDACPL = 9. _____
Calm; quiet

10. ITUDLAMET =10. _____
Disfigured beyond repair

11. RENTOLLIEAB =11. _____
Unbearable

12. ECUSENSNAT =12. _____
Something, esp. food, that sustains life or health

13. SAFMTHO =13. _____
Units of length equal to six feet

14. IARERP =14. _____
A light, sharp-pointed sword lacking a cutting edge and used only for thrusting

15. TMYUIHLI =15. _____
Marked by meekness or modesty in behavior

Copyrighted

Old Man & The Sea Vocabulary Juggle Letters 4 Answer Key

1. EDFLRU = 1. FURLED
Rolled up and secured to something

2. SDEEIV = 2. DEVISE
To form, plan, or arrange in one's mind; design or contrive

3. OLSIEROTUN = 3. RESOLUTION
Firm determination

4. VEEACSNRG = 4. SCAVENGER
An animal that feeds on decaying matter

5. NSEUEDR = 5. ENDURES
To carry on through despite hardships

6. SIDECRITEN = 6. IRIDESCENT
Producing a display of lustrous, rainbowlike colors

7. CPHOOEHPEESCRNS = 7. PHOSPHORESCENCE
Emission of light without burning

8. TTPMEONC = 8. CONTEMPT
Scorn; disparaging or haughty disdain

9. IDACPL = 9. PLACID
Calm; quiet

10. ITUDLAMET =10. MUTILATED
Disfigured beyond repair

11. RENTOLLIEAB =11. INTOLERABLE
Unbearable

12. ECUSENSNAT =12. SUSTENANCE
Something, esp. food, that sustains life or health

13. SAFMTHO =13. FATHOMS
Units of length equal to six feet

14. IARERP =14. RAPIER
A light, sharp-pointed sword lacking a cutting edge and used only for thrusting

15. TMYUIHLI =15. HUMILITY
Marked by meekness or modesty in behavior

ATTAINED	Gained as an objective; achieved
BENEVOLENT	Characterized by or suggestive of doing good
COMMENCED	Began; started
CONGREGATED	Gathered; assembled
CONTEMPT	Scorn; disparaging or haughty disdain
CONVULSIVELY	Shaking or agitating violently with irregular and involuntary muscular contractions

DEVISE	To form, plan, or arrange in one's mind; design or contrive
ENDURES	To carry on through despite hardships
FATHOMS	Units of length equal to six feet
FURLED	Rolled up and secured to something
HUMILIATING	Lowering the pride, dignity or self-respect
HUMILITY	Marked by meekness or modesty in behavior

IMMUNE	Not affected by a given influence; unresponsive
INEFFECTUAL	Insufficient to produce a desired effect
INTOLERABLE	Unbearable
IRIDESCENT	Producing a display of lustrous, rainbowlike colors
MALIGNANCY	Something disposed to do evil; highly injurious
MUTILATED	Disfigured beyond repair

PHOSPHORESCENCE	Emission of light without burning
PLACID	Calm; quiet
PROLONGS	To lengthen in duration; protract
RAPIER	A light, sharp-pointed sword lacking a cutting edge and used only for thrusting
RESOLUTION	Firm determination
SCAVENGER	An animal that feeds on decaying matter

SUSTENANCE	Something, esp. food, that sustains life or health
THWART	A seat across a boat on which a rower may sit
VIOLATED	Broke or disregarded

Old Man & The Sea Vocabulary

INTOLERABLE	IRIDESCENT	ENDURES	DEVISE	FATHOMS
RESOLUTION	THWART	CONTEMPT	PROLONGS	COMMENCED
VIOLATED	BENEVOLENT	FREE SPACE	ATTAINED	MALIGNANCY
INEFFECTUAL	CONGREGATED	CONVULSIVELY	HUMILIATING	SCAVENGER
HUMILITY	FURLED	PHOSPHORESCENCE	MUTILATED	RAPIER

Old Man & The Sea Vocabulary

IMMUNE	SUSTENANCE	RAPIER	MUTILATED	PHOSPHORESCENCE
FURLED	HUMILITY	SCAVENGER	HUMILIATING	CONVULSIVELY
CONGREGATED	INEFFECTUAL	FREE SPACE	ATTAINED	PLACID
BENEVOLENT	VIOLATED	COMMENCED	PROLONGS	CONTEMPT
THWART	RESOLUTION	FATHOMS	DEVISE	ENDURES

Old Man & The Sea Vocabulary

DEVISE	CONVULSIVELY	FURLED	HUMILITY	BENEVOLENT
IRIDESCENT	FATHOMS	MALIGNANCY	HUMILIATING	SUSTENANCE
CONGREGATED	ATTAINED	FREE SPACE	INEFFECTUAL	PHOSPHORESCENCE
IMMUNE	CONTEMPT	COMMENCED	PLACID	RAPIER
INTOLERABLE	THWART	MUTILATED	VIOLATED	SCAVENGER

Old Man & The Sea Vocabulary

RESOLUTION	ENDURES	SCAVENGER	VIOLATED	MUTILATED
THWART	INTOLERABLE	RAPIER	PLACID	COMMENCED
CONTEMPT	IMMUNE	FREE SPACE	INEFFECTUAL	PROLONGS
ATTAINED	CONGREGATED	SUSTENANCE	HUMILIATING	MALIGNANCY
FATHOMS	IRIDESCENT	BENEVOLENT	HUMILITY	FURLED

Old Man & The Sea Vocabulary

PHOSPHORESCENCE	INEFFECTUAL	CONTEMPT	PROLONGS	THWART
IMMUNE	MUTILATED	HUMILITY	DEVISE	ATTAINED
MALIGNANCY	BENEVOLENT	FREE SPACE	FATHOMS	RAPIER
HUMILIATING	COMMENCED	IRIDESCENT	SUSTENANCE	RESOLUTION
CONVULSIVELY	SCAVENGER	PLACID	VIOLATED	FURLED

Old Man & The Sea Vocabulary

INTOLERABLE	ENDURES	FURLED	VIOLATED	PLACID
SCAVENGER	CONVULSIVELY	RESOLUTION	SUSTENANCE	IRIDESCENT
COMMENCED	HUMILIATING	FREE SPACE	FATHOMS	CONGREGATED
BENEVOLENT	MALIGNANCY	ATTAINED	DEVISE	HUMILITY
MUTILATED	IMMUNE	THWART	PROLONGS	CONTEMPT

Old Man & The Sea Vocabulary

PROLONGS	RESOLUTION	RAPIER	SUSTENANCE	HUMILIATING
MALIGNANCY	ENDURES	IRIDESCENT	DEVISE	INEFFECTUAL
THWART	IMMUNE	FREE SPACE	PLACID	CONVULSIVELY
BENEVOLENT	ATTAINED	CONTEMPT	INTOLERABLE	PHOSPHORESCENCE
VIOLATED	SCAVENGER	FURLED	FATHOMS	MUTILATED

Old Man & The Sea Vocabulary

HUMILITY	CONGREGATED	MUTILATED	FATHOMS	FURLED
SCAVENGER	VIOLATED	PHOSPHORESCENCE	INTOLERABLE	CONTEMPT
ATTAINED	BENEVOLENT	FREE SPACE	PLACID	COMMENCED
IMMUNE	THWART	INEFFECTUAL	DEVISE	IRIDESCENT
ENDURES	MALIGNANCY	HUMILIATING	SUSTENANCE	RAPIER

Old Man & The Sea Vocabulary

SCAVENGER	HUMILIATING	RAPIER	ATTAINED	FATHOMS
RESOLUTION	FURLED	IRIDESCENT	CONGREGATED	PLACID
CONVULSIVELY	COMMENCED	FREE SPACE	IMMUNE	HUMILITY
INEFFECTUAL	ENDURES	PROLONGS	INTOLERABLE	SUSTENANCE
CONTEMPT	VIOLATED	BENEVOLENT	MUTILATED	DEVISE

Old Man & The Sea Vocabulary

THWART	MALIGNANCY	DEVISE	MUTILATED	BENEVOLENT
VIOLATED	CONTEMPT	SUSTENANCE	INTOLERABLE	PROLONGS
ENDURES	INEFFECTUAL	FREE SPACE	IMMUNE	PHOSPHORESCENCE
COMMENCED	CONVULSIVELY	PLACID	CONGREGATED	IRIDESCENT
FURLED	RESOLUTION	FATHOMS	ATTAINED	RAPIER

Old Man & The Sea Vocabulary

INTOLERABLE	BENEVOLENT	ATTAINED	INEFFECTUAL	HUMILITY
MUTILATED	CONVULSIVELY	PHOSPHORESCENCE	CONGREGATED	IRIDESCENT
COMMENCED	CONTEMPT	FREE SPACE	IMMUNE	THWART
ENDURES	RAPIER	RESOLUTION	HUMILIATING	PROLONGS
SCAVENGER	VIOLATED	SUSTENANCE	DEVISE	MALIGNANCY

Old Man & The Sea Vocabulary

PLACID	FATHOMS	MALIGNANCY	DEVISE	SUSTENANCE
VIOLATED	SCAVENGER	PROLONGS	HUMILIATING	RESOLUTION
RAPIER	ENDURES	FREE SPACE	IMMUNE	FURLED
CONTEMPT	COMMENCED	IRIDESCENT	CONGREGATED	PHOSPHORESCENCE
CONVULSIVELY	MUTILATED	HUMILITY	INEFFECTUAL	ATTAINED

Old Man & The Sea Vocabulary

IRIDESCENT	DEVISE	PROLONGS	SUSTENANCE	FURLED
RESOLUTION	IMMUNE	VIOLATED	FATHOMS	SCAVENGER
RAPIER	CONVULSIVELY	FREE SPACE	COMMENCED	MALIGNANCY
HUMILITY	INTOLERABLE	BENEVOLENT	CONTEMPT	ATTAINED
PHOSPHORESCENCE	ENDURES	HUMILIATING	THWART	CONGREGATED

Old Man & The Sea Vocabulary

MUTILATED	PLACID	CONGREGATED	THWART	HUMILIATING
ENDURES	PHOSPHORESCENCE	ATTAINED	CONTEMPT	BENEVOLENT
INTOLERABLE	HUMILITY	FREE SPACE	COMMENCED	INEFFECTUAL
CONVULSIVELY	RAPIER	SCAVENGER	FATHOMS	VIOLATED
IMMUNE	RESOLUTION	FURLED	SUSTENANCE	PROLONGS

Old Man & The Sea Vocabulary

HUMILIATING	CONGREGATED	MUTILATED	BENEVOLENT	MALIGNANCY
FATHOMS	DEVISE	VIOLATED	PROLONGS	ATTAINED
SCAVENGER	PHOSPHORESCENCE	FREE SPACE	CONVULSIVELY	CONTEMPT
HUMILITY	SUSTENANCE	IMMUNE	INEFFECTUAL	COMMENCED
PLACID	RAPIER	FURLED	RESOLUTION	ENDURES

Old Man & The Sea Vocabulary

THWART	IRIDESCENT	ENDURES	RESOLUTION	FURLED
RAPIER	PLACID	COMMENCED	INEFFECTUAL	IMMUNE
SUSTENANCE	HUMILITY	FREE SPACE	CONVULSIVELY	INTOLERABLE
PHOSPHORESCENCE	SCAVENGER	ATTAINED	PROLONGS	VIOLATED
DEVISE	FATHOMS	MALIGNANCY	BENEVOLENT	MUTILATED

Old Man & The Sea Vocabulary

CONVULSIVELY	BENEVOLENT	ATTAINED	HUMILITY	ENDURES
PHOSPHORESCENCE	RESOLUTION	IMMUNE	MALIGNANCY	HUMILIATING
RAPIER	CONGREGATED	FREE SPACE	PROLONGS	IRIDESCENT
THWART	INTOLERABLE	VIOLATED	SCAVENGER	PLACID
SUSTENANCE	FURLED	FATHOMS	COMMENCED	DEVISE

Old Man & The Sea Vocabulary

CONTEMPT	INEFFECTUAL	DEVISE	COMMENCED	FATHOMS
FURLED	SUSTENANCE	PLACID	SCAVENGER	VIOLATED
INTOLERABLE	THWART	FREE SPACE	PROLONGS	MUTILATED
CONGREGATED	RAPIER	HUMILIATING	MALIGNANCY	IMMUNE
RESOLUTION	PHOSPHORESCENCE	ENDURES	HUMILITY	ATTAINED

Old Man & The Sea Vocabulary

RESOLUTION	SCAVENGER	THWART	HUMILIATING	BENEVOLENT
FURLED	VIOLATED	CONVULSIVELY	COMMENCED	DEVISE
IRIDESCENT	RAPIER	FREE SPACE	PROLONGS	INTOLERABLE
ATTAINED	CONGREGATED	MALIGNANCY	CONTEMPT	PLACID
SUSTENANCE	FATHOMS	HUMILITY	INEFFECTUAL	IMMUNE

Old Man & The Sea Vocabulary

ENDURES	PHOSPHORESCENCE	IMMUNE	INEFFECTUAL	HUMILITY
FATHOMS	SUSTENANCE	PLACID	CONTEMPT	MALIGNANCY
CONGREGATED	ATTAINED	FREE SPACE	PROLONGS	MUTILATED
RAPIER	IRIDESCENT	DEVISE	COMMENCED	CONVULSIVELY
VIOLATED	FURLED	BENEVOLENT	HUMILIATING	THWART

Old Man & The Sea Vocabulary

CONVULSIVELY	RAPIER	IRIDESCENT	VIOLATED	FATHOMS
INEFFECTUAL	COMMENCED	ENDURES	BENEVOLENT	IMMUNE
DEVISE	RESOLUTION	FREE SPACE	MUTILATED	THWART
ATTAINED	FURLED	SCAVENGER	PLACID	CONGREGATED
MALIGNANCY	CONTEMPT	PROLONGS	SUSTENANCE	PHOSPHORESCENCE

Old Man & The Sea Vocabulary

INTOLERABLE	HUMILIATING	PHOSPHORESCENCE	SUSTENANCE	PROLONGS
CONTEMPT	MALIGNANCY	CONGREGATED	PLACID	SCAVENGER
FURLED	ATTAINED	FREE SPACE	MUTILATED	HUMILITY
RESOLUTION	DEVISE	IMMUNE	BENEVOLENT	ENDURES
COMMENCED	INEFFECTUAL	FATHOMS	VIOLATED	IRIDESCENT

Old Man & The Sea Vocabulary

VIOLATED	ATTAINED	PROLONGS	CONGREGATED	HUMILIATING
FATHOMS	BENEVOLENT	ENDURES	HUMILITY	INEFFECTUAL
IMMUNE	IRIDESCENT	FREE SPACE	MALIGNANCY	RESOLUTION
FURLED	COMMENCED	MUTILATED	CONVULSIVELY	SCAVENGER
PLACID	INTOLERABLE	RAPIER	THWART	DEVISE

Old Man & The Sea Vocabulary

SUSTENANCE	PHOSPHORESCENCE	DEVISE	THWART	RAPIER
INTOLERABLE	PLACID	SCAVENGER	CONVULSIVELY	MUTILATED
COMMENCED	FURLED	FREE SPACE	MALIGNANCY	CONTEMPT
IRIDESCENT	IMMUNE	INEFFECTUAL	HUMILITY	ENDURES
BENEVOLENT	FATHOMS	HUMILIATING	CONGREGATED	PROLONGS

Old Man & The Sea Vocabulary

CONTEMPT	MUTILATED	RAPIER	ENDURES	FURLED
HUMILITY	CONVULSIVELY	VIOLATED	DEVISE	CONGREGATED
HUMILIATING	FATHOMS	FREE SPACE	BENEVOLENT	INEFFECTUAL
IMMUNE	THWART	PHOSPHORESCENCE	COMMENCED	SCAVENGER
MALIGNANCY	INTOLERABLE	ATTAINED	SUSTENANCE	PROLONGS

Old Man & The Sea Vocabulary

PLACID	RESOLUTION	PROLONGS	SUSTENANCE	ATTAINED
INTOLERABLE	MALIGNANCY	SCAVENGER	COMMENCED	PHOSPHORESCENCE
THWART	IMMUNE	FREE SPACE	BENEVOLENT	IRIDESCENT
FATHOMS	HUMILIATING	CONGREGATED	DEVISE	VIOLATED
CONVULSIVELY	HUMILITY	FURLED	ENDURES	RAPIER

Old Man & The Sea Vocabulary

SUSTENANCE	RESOLUTION	CONTEMPT	FATHOMS	DEVISE
INEFFECTUAL	CONGREGATED	HUMILITY	COMMENCED	INTOLERABLE
PHOSPHORESCENCE	IMMUNE	FREE SPACE	ATTAINED	RAPIER
CONVULSIVELY	PROLONGS	MALIGNANCY	ENDURES	HUMILIATING
FURLED	SCAVENGER	THWART	PLACID	VIOLATED

Old Man & The Sea Vocabulary

IRIDESCENT	MUTILATED	VIOLATED	PLACID	THWART
SCAVENGER	FURLED	HUMILIATING	ENDURES	MALIGNANCY
PROLONGS	CONVULSIVELY	FREE SPACE	ATTAINED	BENEVOLENT
IMMUNE	PHOSPHORESCENCE	INTOLERABLE	COMMENCED	HUMILITY
CONGREGATED	INEFFECTUAL	DEVISE	FATHOMS	CONTEMPT

Old Man & The Sea Vocabulary

INEFFECTUAL	MUTILATED	SUSTENANCE	SCAVENGER	PLACID
HUMILITY	ENDURES	PROLONGS	MALIGNANCY	PHOSPHORESCENCE
DEVISE	THWART	FREE SPACE	CONVULSIVELY	IRIDESCENT
ATTAINED	CONGREGATED	CONTEMPT	VIOLATED	BENEVOLENT
RAPIER	HUMILIATING	FATHOMS	INTOLERABLE	IMMUNE

Old Man & The Sea Vocabulary

RESOLUTION	COMMENCED	IMMUNE	INTOLERABLE	FATHOMS
HUMILIATING	RAPIER	BENEVOLENT	VIOLATED	CONTEMPT
CONGREGATED	ATTAINED	FREE SPACE	CONVULSIVELY	FURLED
THWART	DEVISE	PHOSPHORESCENCE	MALIGNANCY	PROLONGS
ENDURES	HUMILITY	PLACID	SCAVENGER	SUSTENANCE

Old Man & The Sea Vocabulary

SCAVENGER	RAPIER	CONTEMPT	CONVULSIVELY	VIOLATED
BENEVOLENT	IRIDESCENT	THWART	ATTAINED	MUTILATED
COMMENCED	CONGREGATED	FREE SPACE	SUSTENANCE	ENDURES
PROLONGS	DEVISE	FURLED	HUMILITY	RESOLUTION
IMMUNE	INEFFECTUAL	HUMILIATING	FATHOMS	INTOLERABLE

Old Man & The Sea Vocabulary

MALIGNANCY	PHOSPHORESCENCE	INTOLERABLE	FATHOMS	HUMILIATING
INEFFECTUAL	IMMUNE	RESOLUTION	HUMILITY	FURLED
DEVISE	PROLONGS	FREE SPACE	SUSTENANCE	PLACID
CONGREGATED	COMMENCED	MUTILATED	ATTAINED	THWART
IRIDESCENT	BENEVOLENT	VIOLATED	CONVULSIVELY	CONTEMPT